POLICY STUDIES IN EMPLOYMENT AND WELFARE NUMBER 34

General Editor: Sar A. Levitan

More Than Subsistence:
Minimum Wages
for the Working Poor

Sar A. Levitan
and
Richard S. Belous

The Johns Hopkins University Press
Baltimore and London

This study was prepared under a grant from the Ford Foundation.

Graphics by Patrick D. Zickler

The Johns Hopkins University Press, Baltimore, Maryland 21218
The Johns Hopkins Press Ltd., London

Library of Congress Catalog Number 79–11688

ISBN 0–8018–2251–3
ISBN 0–8018–2274–2 (pbk.)

Library of Congress Cataloging in Publication data
will be found on the last printed page of this book.

Contents

Preface

Horatio Alger rags-to-riches stories are no longer in vogue, but our nation still clings to the notion that good old honest work is the solution to poverty. Would that it were so. The truth is that there are not enough jobs for all who want them. Indeed, some economists continue to preach that there is a "natural rate" of unemployment. The statistical sleight of hand has gone so far that one former chief presidential economic adviser pronounced that "full employment" may exist in the United States when 7 million jobless people are looking for work.

Even if a job can be found, employment is no sure escape from poverty. It is a commentary on our income distribution system that for millions of Americans the rewards from work are too meager to eradicate poverty. Yet, although work has not been the salvation for millions of poverty-stricken families, the poor have shown an almost amazing propensity—given the circumstances and the low rewards—to work.

Welfare, training, and other remedial government programs do little for the working poor. To date, the minimum wage has been the most direct and comprehensive policy tool designed to help improve their lot. The minimum wage remains a controversial piece of social legislation as Congress continues to change the level of the minimum wage, keeping it close to half of the average wage. Issues related to the minimum wage are hot political items. For example, during the 1977 round of congressional amendments a proposal to create a subminimum wage for teenage workers lost in the House by only one vote—that of the Speaker, who broke a tie.

Few government policies have been run through more statistical and econometric tests than the wage floor. In fact, minimum wage research provides an excellent case study of how the dismal science is practiced in the United States today. Despite all the advanced techniques and technology, few hard-and-fast quantitative results have been obtained. Studies conducted by respectable practitioners of the art have come down on all sides of the issue. Even the researchers who agree on the basic direction of the minimum wage impacts have differed, and sometimes sharply, on the magnitude of these results.

One of the prime motives behind this study has been to examine what the econometric calculations and computer simulations have wrought. Going through the models, equations, regressions, statistical proxies, and dummy variables, it becomes clear that backing up the "objective" scientific results are the researchers' assumptions, biases, and value judgments—more frequently obfuscated, if not hidden, than clearly spelled out.

Granted these complications, a strong case can be made that the minimum wage has served a highly beneficial function. The negative spillovers caused by the minimum wage are too frequently overstated. Even in the case of teenagers, the social costs do not appear to be unmanageable. The econometric evidence—stripped of hidden assumptions—indicates that the wage floor cannot even begin to explain the youth unemployment problem during the 1960s and 1970s. Pointing a finger at the minimum wage as the prime cause may be a favorite pastime of some, but it just is not supported by the facts.

Reluctance to utilize the minimum wage to maintain the well-being of the working poor is not based on documentation of massive job losses or inflationary pressures. There is no proof that the minimum wage has caused massive problems, and there is a great deal of evidence supporting its positive contributions to society, as millions of working poor might have remained even more deprived without government intervention. A second conclusion derived from this study is that it is high time to reexamine the impact of the "new technology" on the social sciences. The lofty claims of the numerologists have not been justified by recent experience.

Traditional economic theory can be a very powerful tool of anaylsis, and it can provide real insight into many complex social relationships. However, these standard tools will not provide a full picture of events if an analyst does not consider the institutional environment of the period being studied. The problem, we feel, is that many aspects of the minimum wage have not been considered in research condemning the current wage floor program. At issue are not the motives of neo-classical economists. The central difference involves scope, emphasis, and methodology.

This study tries to go beyond the standard analysis of minimum wages and employment effects. The goal is to consider the role of the wage floor and basic attitudes toward work in a mature welfare state. Minimum wages, as is all too often the case, are measured against some ideal situation—perfect competition, say—and found wanting. A useful and unbiased assessment of the wage floor must consider the realistic policy alternatives—not ideal conditions or the dreams and biases of economists. Reliance upon work for support of the unskilled and deficiently educated, in the realm of the welfare state, will become increasingly difficult without an effective wage floor. This nation may worship at the shrine of the work ethic, but many employers have tried to purchase this devotion at a very cheap price.

This study reviews the general role of the minimum wage in relation to the working poor and the welfare state. It then traces the history of the wage floor from the early reform campaigns at the turn of the century to the current era of the Fair Labor Standards Act. Next it examines the statistical and econometric research on the wage floor. The prime goal is not to survey specific findings, but rather to examine the different research methods that have been employed. Using the 1977 round of congressional amendments as a case study, the volume examines various minimum wage policy options. The study closes with a summary of the statistical and historical evidence and a consideration of alternative policy tools. The story of minimum wage research is far from finished, but we have reached a point at which some tentative conclusions can be drawn.

We are indebted to Charles T. Stewart, Jr., and Robert S. Goldfarb, both of the George Washington University, Jack I. Karlin, U.S. Department of Labor, and Joyce K. Zickler, Federal Reserve, for their helpful critical comments. This study was prepared under a grant from the Ford Foundation to the George Washington University's Center for Social Policy Studies. In accordance with the foundation's practice, responsibility for the content was left completely to the authors.

More Than Subsistence

1

The Role of Minimum Wages

The Persistence of Low Wages

A job—even full-time employment— is no sure escape from poverty. The image of the destitute, idling through life on welfare or eking out a living from old-age receipts, is far from a total picture of real conditions within our society.

When considering poverty or the "welfare mess," politicians, journalists, and other citizens often bemoan the alleged demise of the work ethic. It is asserted that if those in the poverty ranks would turn away from welfare and readjust themselves to a steady diet of workfare, poverty could be eliminated or at least vastly reduced. This pervasive notion fails to take into consideration several overriding facts concerning our economy.

First, the economy is not now, nor has it often been in the past, able to generate enough employment opportunities for all Americans. The goal of full employment appears distant and, to an increasing number of economic analysts, unattainable. The recent influx of large numbers of undocumented aliens, frequently com-

1

peting with citizens for scarce jobs, makes the achievement of full employment, or tight labor markets, even more elusive. Also, historically high labor force participation rates complicate reaching this goal.

Second, millions of people in the poverty ranks are already working! Being employed full time does not necessarily mean an individual or a family is receiving an income large enough to escape poverty. Millions of family heads are active workers but still can not support their familes at a minimally acceptable level above the formally recognized poverty threshold. The United States also is the only advanced industrialized nation without a family allowance program.

As long as the supply of unskilled and deficiently educated labor exceeds the demand for marginal work, it should not be surprising that by any standard the poverty population will contain a relatively high percentage of working poor. The Hobson's choice facing this group is not one of work *or* poverty; the harsh reality is work *and* poverty. The problems of the working poor are more fundamental than the impact of a recession or temporary cyclical unemployment. For many unemployment is a relatively short-term experience; yet the hardship of the working poor can often be a way of life. The long-term labor market difficulties of the working poor linger even in boom times.

The persistence of poverty for many active members of the American labor force testifies to the maldistribution of societal rewards for work and the need for improvement. But the plight of the working poor in the past has received scant attention in governmental antirecession and poverty programs. Training, welfare, and public employment efforts tend to be preoccupied with the unemployed, youth, and those outside of the labor force. The goal of most training programs is full-time employment for the unemployed. That this may be only a partial solution to poverty is often ignored, as are the needs of those who are already laboring at full-time, low-paying jobs.

Protection of the Working Poor

The minimum wage is the most direct and comprehensive measure to increase the earnings of the working poor. The objective of the Fair Labor Standards Act of 1938 (FLSA) was to achieve, as rapidly as practicable, minimum wage levels that would sustain the health, efficiency, and general well-being of all workers without eliminating too many jobs. Minimum wage legislation, in general, involves setting a floor on wage rates. Private and public employers covered by the legislation are not permitted to hire workers at below a specified hourly wage rate. On the assumption that a low-paying job is better than no job at all, Congress has acted incrementally in applying the law over the years. Historically, it has established minimum wages that directly affect only a limited number of employees at the bottom of the economic ladder. When the minimum wage was raised to $2.90 an hour in 1979, 5.1 million workers received direct pay increases.

About 54 million nonsupervisory employees—almost 80 percent of nonsupervisory workers—were covered in September 1977 by the minimum wage provisions of the FLSA (Figure 1). In the mining, construction, manufacturing, transportation and public utilities, wholesale and finance, and insurance and real estate industries, nearly all workers not in supervisory positions are covered. Although all nonsupervisory employees in the federal government are covered, a 1976 Supreme Court decision removed minimum wage protection for many state and local government employees. Almost equal percentages of females and males are covered by these minimum wage provisions. Even when compared by race, differences are small between coverage of males and females.[1]

About 11.5 million workers in nonsupervisory positions are exempt from the minimum wage and/or overtime provisions of the FLSA. Roughly 7.7 million of these uncovered positions are in the private sector, and they are concentrated in retail and service

3

Figure 1.   More than three out of five wage and salary workers are covered by the minimum wage (September 1977).

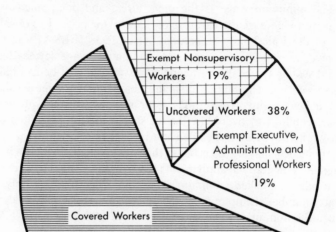

Source: U.S. Department of Labor.

industries (Figure 2). In Puerto Rico more than nine-tenths of the island's nonsupervisory employees (excluding outside sales workers) are covered by minimum wage provisions of the FLSA.[2] State minimum wage laws provide protection to some workers exempt from FLSA, but these standards range widely.

The minimum wage remains a controversial piece of social legislation as Congress continues to expand coverage and raise the floor so that it remains at about half the average wage paid in the manufacturing sector. With such a large percentage of the labor

4

Figure 2. Many workers who need the protection most are not covered by the minimum wage.

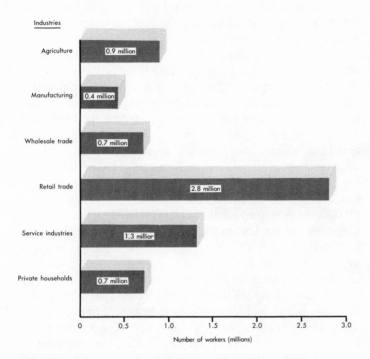

Industries

Source: U.S. Department of Labor.

force covered by the FLSA and with so many firms working under its provisions, it might be natural to expect that minimum wage opponents would be almost as extinct as the advocates of a return to the gold standard. However, this is not the case. While the disputes surrounding this living document have come a long way from the initial rate of 25 cents per hour, the minimum wage remains possibly as controversial now as the day Congress first enacted the FLSA.[3] A 1966 survey found that 61 percent of university economists and 79 percent of business economists opposed

5

amendments to increase and broaden the coverage of the minimum wage.[4]

Robert S. Goldfarb, an economist who has studied the impact of minimum wages, has described the problems of reaching well-grounded statistical conclusions.[5] Few, if any, federal acts have been the subject of more economic analysis than the minimum wage and its impact on labor markets and the economy as a whole. But broadly accepted and statistically grounded conclusions concerning the basic impacts of minimum wages remain elusive.

Consider the impact of minimum wages on employment, which might be the most susceptible to measurement. During 1977 congressional hearings on proposed amendments to the minimum wage lawmakers were assured by Secretary of Labor Ray Marshall, a trained and prominent labor economist, that the number of jobs lost because of a boost in the minimum wage would be only 90,000. At the same time the chief economist for the Chamber of Commerce of the United States concluded that the employment loss would be over 830,000 jobs.[6] And each side marshalled the evidence to prove its claim.

However, bias is not the prime reason for such a wide range in the estimates or for the dearth of predictions that land in roughly the same ball park. This condition reflects both the advances and the problems of complex statistical and econometric research undertaken by the dismal science. In fact, the minimum wage studies provide a classic case of how economists operate, and they demonstrate both the strengths and the weaknesses of what ordinarily passes as economic analysis. Hence, the research in minimum wage offers a very good case study of the status of economics as it is currently practiced in the United States.

Since analysts both pro and con on the minimum wage tend to hinge their arguments on its net impact on the working poor, we should first know more about this sizable segment of society. Only then can one attempt to measure the benefits and cost of the minimum wage.

Poverty among the Working Poor

Many of the jobs held by the working poor have a high turnover rate, partly because they are very low-wage, dead-end jobs. Such employment often provides neither security nor earnings adequate to stabilize employment patterns. Given this lack of stability, traditional labor force concepts fail to describe satisfactorily the conditions within these labor markets. The same working poor person who may be counted in the labor force one day might be out of the official labor force the next. An analysis of the minimum wage involves, therefore, an examination of the entire destitute population who are frequently the victims of low wages.

There were approximately 25 million people below the poverty level in 1976, constituting 11.8 percent of the entire United States population. These figures represent both a relative and an absolute decline in the poverty population since 1959, when about 39.5 million people, or 22.4 percent of Americans, were counted as poor (Figure 3). The distribution of poverty is far from uniform within our society when considered on the basis of sex, race, ethnic origin, geography, or age. For example, a female-headed family has about five times greater a chance of being in poverty than a male-headed family. Besides a higher incidence of poverty among female-headed families, blacks and Hispanics also experience a high relative rate of poverty. In 1976 more than 7.5 million blacks —31.1 percent of the entire black population—lived in poverty, compared with 9.1 percent of the white population and 24.7 percent of Hispanics.

Who Can Work?

Of the roughly 25 million Americans in poverty, it would be unrealistic to expect that the majority can or should work. About half of the poverty population is under the age of 16 or 65 years of age or older.

Figure 3. Despite improvements, nearly 12 percent of the American people still live in poverty.

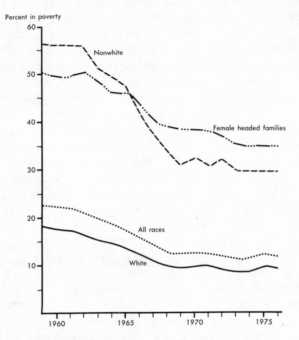

Source: U.S. Department of Commerce, Bureau of the Census.

Many destitute individuals are beset with numerous problems blocking an active worklife. Nearly one of every ten poor individuals is either too ill or too disabled to hold down a working position. At the same time, 3.9 million destitute people did not work in 1976 because of housekeeping and family obligations. It is difficult to estimate a specific figure that represents the correct number of poor people who can or should be working. Housekeeping, family obligations, going to school, and even being ill or disabled can not always be taken as absolute indications of ability

8

to enter the labor market. The question of whether a person is in the labor force depends upon many variables, including job opportunities, the level of wages and other benefits, the general level of unemployment, family income, and government regulations. Specially targeted employment and training efforts could expand with opportunities for partially ill and disabled individuals. Yet this would raise the question of displacement. Also, different regulations could change the number of people below the poverty level who remain outside the work force because of housekeeping obligations.

A reasonable estimate would suggest that roughly 7 million people aged 16 years and over within the poverty population, or about 28 percent, could be considered potential candidates for the ranks of the American labor force.

Measuring Poverty

A poverty rate of close to 12 percent of the entire population for the world's richest and one of its most productive economies connotes institutional shortcomings and should be a cause for concern. And yet it could be argued that, although we should do more in fighting economic deprivation, the notion of poverty is in part a relative concept. Poverty can be defined as a lack of goods and services needed for an adequate standard of living. Because standards of adequacy vary both with a society's general level of well-being and with public attitudes toward deprivation, there is no universally accepted definition of individual or family basic needs. The amount of money income required to provide for an agreed-upon set of basic needs is equally difficult to determine.

Despite these conceptual and technical problems of measurement, the federal government has devised a poverty index that has gained wide acceptance. This index reflects the different consumption requirements of families based on size and composition, sex and age of the family head, and farm or nonfarm residence.

Based on survey findings that families of three or more persons spend approximately one-third of their income on food, the poverty level was set at three times the cost of a basic economy food plan. For smaller families and persons living alone, the cost of the basic economy food plan was multiplied by higher factors in order to compensate for the relatively larger fixed expenses of smaller households. The poverty thresholds are updated every year to reflect changes in the Consumer Price Index (CPI) but not overall rises in the standard of living.[7] The poverty threshold for 1979 was as follows:

Number of family members	Nonfarm	Farm
1	$3,400	$2,910
2	4,500	3,840
3	5,600	4,770
4	6,700	5,700
5	7,800	6,630
6	8,900	7,560

Alternative definitions and concepts have a major impact on the poverty estimates. For example, the Congressional Budget Office (CBO) has estimated that in the absence of government transfer payments about 25 percent of all American families would have been in poverty during 1976. However, government cash transfers are included in the official poverty index, and this inclusion reduced the proportion of destitute Americans to roughly 12 percent. If in-kind programs are included, such as subsidized housing and food stamps, then the percentage in poverty may have been reduced even further.[8] But it is fair to say that in the absence of statutory minimum wages, this percentage would have been higher.

Poverty and Work

The paradox of poverty existing in an affluent society is but one dilemma facing the American economy. A second irony is the relatively large number of poor persons who are in the labor force. About 6.6 million people with incomes below the poverty level worked during 1976. Among the working poor were over 4 million people who worked full time and about 2.6 million who had part-time employment. For many heads of familes, working is no solution to the problem of pulling a family out of poverty. About 2.5 million working heads of families still remained below the poverty level—nearly one of ten working family heads. Included among the working poor were about 1 million heads of families who worked at full-time, full-year jobs.

Breaking this down by sex, 85 percent of poor male heads work, and 29 percent work full time, year round. The number of working poor females is also high. About 49 percent of poor female family heads work during the year, and 8 percent work full time, year round. The work experience of the poor was significant (even in the slow recovery during 1976), as is seen when the population is subdivided as follows:[9]

	Total poverty population	White poor	Black poor	Hispanic poor
	(Numbers in (thousands)			
Worked during year	6,555	4,794	1,568	608
Worked 50 to 52 weeks	2,012	1,503	451	138
Worked 49 weeks or less	4,542	3,290	1,117	470

Beyond employment and unemployment statistics there is the question of how many Americans can not meet basic needs of income levels through work.

Economic hardship depends upon an individual's ability to find employment, the wages paid, and family income. Looking at all of these factors that can cause economic hardship, millions of workers have a strong attachment to the labor force (say, 40 weeks or more), earn less than the annualized minimum wage ($4,784 in 1977), and are members of families with an income less that 150 percent of the poverty level. In 1977 the percentages of females

11

and nonwhites in this labor force and family income bind were even higher:[10]

	Both Sexes		Male		Female	
	Number (thousands)	Percent	Number (thousands)	Percent	Number (thousands)	Percent
All groups	5,101	6.6	2,921	5.8	2,184	8.2
White	3,769	5.5	2,259	5.0	1,510	6.7
Black	1,210	15.4	573	12.8	638	18.8
Hispanic	401	9.4	253	10.3	148	12.3
Other	126	9.4	89	10.6	37	7.3

About 4 percent of all husband-and-wife families are in the position of having low wages and low family income; about 15 percent of all female-headed families experience such conditions.

To be sure, there are major differences between the working characteristics of the poor and the rest of society. For example, considering family heads at all income levels, about 6.2 percent were unemployed for 15 weeks or more in 1975. However, 15.2 percent of the heads of poverty families were long-term unemployed having experienced forced idleness of 15 weeks or more.

There are variations in the working characteristics of the poor and the nonpoor, but the work commitment on the part of the poor—given the low remuneration—is surprisingly strong (Figure 4). Many of the poor families also have more than one bread-winner. Nearly one in nine poor families had two wage earners at some time during the year, and close to 4 percent had three or more wage earners during the year. About 13 percent of all mothers living in poverty worked, and more than one-third of poor black mothers worked.

Roughly three of five poverty families depend on some wage earnings to get by; only about one of ten poverty families exists solely on wage earnings. In 1976 the mean family income for poverty families that existed on only their earnings was $3,205 per year, or about 55 percent of the poverty threshold.

Many destitute families had incomes other than earnings from work or from in-kind public assistance. Government transfer payments have more than quadrupled during the decade ending in 1978, and they constitute one-sixth of total disposable personal income available to the American people. But, popular opinions to the contrary, the vast majority of these transfer payments are not made to the poor or even the near poor. In fact, "welfare" spending accounts for less than a fifth of all income and in-kind support that is currently being distributed to roughly one-third of the population.

Figure 4. A major portion of the poverty population remains in the work force during both good and bad times.

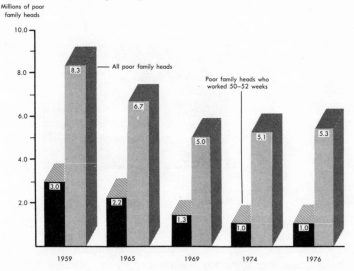

Source: U.S. Department of Commerce, Bureau of the Census.

Despite the fact that work has not been the salvation for millions of poverty families, the poor have shown an almost amazing propensity—given the circumstances and the meager rewards—to work. Many poor families exist on a diet of work and welfare and still remain in poverty.

13

Figure 5. The distribution of hourly earnings demonstrates the clustering of wages near the statutory minimum rate, 1976.

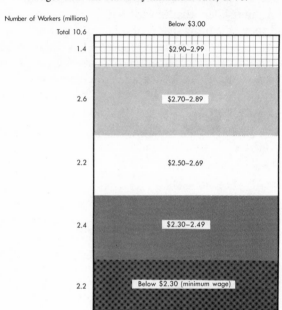

Source: U.S. Department of Labor.

Poverty and Wages

Underemployment and intermittent unemployment are important causes of hardship experienced by the working poor, but low wages must be considered a prime cause of the "work and poverty" paradox. For many in this group even full-time, year-round jobs fail to provide an escape from poverty. The cumulative distribution of wages for employees subject to the federal minimum wage provision in areas other than agriculture and supervisory positions shows the continued prevalence of low-wage workers (Figure 5). The cumulative distribution for farm workers who are

14

subject to the minimum wage provision of the FLSA showed an even lower wage differential than for the nonagricultural sector. At the end of 1976 the cumulative wage distribution for farm workers was as follows:[11]

Average hourly earnings	Number (thousands)	Percent
Total	640	100.0
Under $2.10	98	15.4
Under $2.40	188	29.4
Under $2.70	283	44.2
Under $3.00	343	53.6
$3.00 or over	297	46.4

Even assuming that low-paid workers could secure full-time, 40-hour-per-week jobs and would take no vacations or holidays during an entire year, there still would be millions of American workers who would not be able to bring their families up to or above the poverty threshold. For example, a worker who is the sole supporter of a family of four and who earns the minimum wage would still leave the family below the poverty level. As can be seen from the following hourly wage rates and with the Spartan assumptions listed above, many working poor individuals in a four-member, one-income family would still have incomes placing them under, or just slightly above, the poverty level:

Hourly wage rate	Percentage under or above the poverty level (1978)
$2.65	−11
$2.75	− 8
$2.85	− 4
$3.00	+ 1

But low-wage markets often do not normally provide steady employment; only one out of seven poor family heads worked full time, year round in 1976. Hence, it is correct to assume that in the real world the minimum wage rate would place a worker and his or

15

her family even further below the poverty threshold than indicated by the above simple estimates.

Characteristics of the Working Poor

Personal Characteristics

Besides a higher percentage of blacks, Hispanic Americans, and females, the poverty population also demonstrates other important differences in personal characteristics when compared with the entire population. Some of these differences include educational attainment and place of residence.

Considering the heads of poverty households, about one out of four completed less than eight years of elementary school education; this compares with only one of ten for all household heads. Only one of four poverty family heads finished high school, but roughly one of three heads of all families graduated from high schools. On the basis of age, sex, and race, the working poor show a lower level of educational attainment than the rest of the population.

Place of residence also affects the incidence of poverty. Rural poverty is still endemic. One-third of the entire population lives outside of major metropolitan areas, but this group accounts for one of every two persons living in poverty. The poverty population also is concentrated in certain regions of the country, although the estimates do not consider differences in the cost of living. The distribution in 1976 was as follows:

Region	Total population		Poverty population	
	(millions)	(percent)	(millions)	(percent)
Total	212	100.0	25	100.0
Northeast	49	22.8	5	19.8
North central	57	26.9	6	22.7
South	68	32.1	10	41.1
West	38	18.1	4	16.1

Given these factors, the personal characteristics of low-wage workers show a strong relationship to sex, race, age, educational attainment, and area of residence. These conditions raise the question of whether their wages reflect a low level of productivity or societal biases. The results might represent the failings of our institutions, including labor markets and educational programs.

Industries and Occupations

The jobs held by the working poor tend to be concentrated in selected industries and geographic areas, often in the southern part of the United States. In manufacturing, eight major industrial groups—textile, mill products, apparel, lumber and wood products, furniture and fixtures, rubber and miscellaneous plastic products, leather products, and miscellaneous small manufacturing industries—account for a majority of the low-wage industrial jobs. Retail trade is another major source of low-wage work. Agricultural, service industries, and hospital employment also tend to include a high concentration of low-wage workers.[12] Low-wage industries are most often highly competitive and have numerous and relatively small firms producing products or services that are quite similar.

For these reasons traditional notions that "exploitation of labor" is the culprit accounting for low wages often fail to give a clear picture of real low-wage labor markets. Because of their size and number, very few low-wage firms dominate their labor markets. Also, low-wage industries tend to have below average profit levels, compared with the rest of the economy. This is not to say that exploitation and discrimination have nothing to do with low wages—in fact, they often are the prime causes of low wages. But it is a curious irony of the free market system that those industries that are often the closet approximations of the mythical state of perfect competition are also the same sectors of the economy that contain high percentages of the working poor. Hence, from the

17

individual worker's point of view it often is better to be employed by a firm that has strong (or even monopoly) power over product markets than to be employed by a firm that faces strong competition.

Most low-wage industries spend very little on research and development. High productivity levels in low-wage industries often are the results of research and development and investment undertaken by other high-wage industries, the government, or nonprofit institutions.[13] For example, agriculture has a high concentration of the working poor, and yet agricultural productivity levels often are quite high. However, agricultural productivity gains in many cases appear to have been the result of government-sponsored research and investment and of technological innovations instituted by other industries.

The relationship between productivity and wages is highly important. Some economists still preach that wages paid to workers equal the value of their marginal productivity. For the entire society there is a key relationship between average productivity levels and the average level of real wages, since the recipe for a free lunch has yet to be discovered. It does not follow, however, that individual workers in specific job slots are paid in direct relation to their productivity. The relationships between productivity, low-wage industries, and workers are highly complex and defy simplistic notions and equations.

A low-wage industry can employ many high-paid employees, and many high-wage industries may fill some jobs with low-paid workers. For this reason, it is important to consider the occupations of the working poor as well as the industries in which they most often work.

The working poor tend to be highly concentrated in several broadly defined occupational groupings, including the self-employed, farm workers, cleaning and food service workers, domestic household workers, and laborers. Similarly, race and sex are determinants of low wages, frequently without regard to an

18

individual's productivity (Figure 6). Of the roughly 6 million working poor, about 1.1 million are food service workers, 480,000 are laborers (except farm), 625,000 are domestic workers, 400,000 are farm laborers, and about 980,000 are clerical workers.

Figure 6. The working poor tend to be concentrated in several low-wage occupations.

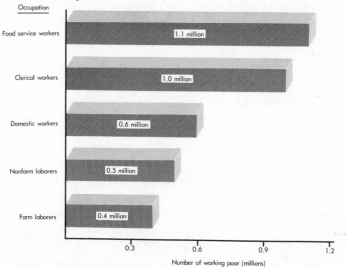

Source: U.S. Department of Commerce, Bureau of the Census.

There often is a strong relationship between the occupational mix of an industry and whether it is a low-wage sector of the economy. Low-wage industries tend to have a higher ratio of production to nonproduction workers, laborers to skilled craftsmen, or clerical to professional and technical employees.

Segmented Labor Markets

Low-wage labor markets often demonstrate characteristics quite different from other types of labor markets, and minimum

19

wages are sometimes viewed as a method for alleviating labor market pathologies. These arguments center on dual or segmented labor market concepts. To understand these concepts, it is necessary first to come to grips with traditional wage and labor demand theories. Traditional economic theory contends that through the workings of labor markets an employee is paid a wage equal to the value of the individual's marginal productivity. There is a sense of "justice" to this notion in that it seems fair that a worker should be compensated in line with the contribution he or she makes to production.

Whatever the equity of the marginal productivity theory, there is little evidence that the real world operates in such fashion. Institutional economists have long rejected the notion that workers are compensated in this manner, even in the long run. More recently, economists have developed dual or segmented labor market concepts, which suggest that economic relationships are often highly complex and imperfect and display numerous institutional rigidities.

In general, the newer concepts hold that—in contrast to traditional theory of the labor market where workers line up in one queue to be selected by employers—there are numerous labor markets. First, there are what may be called the *primary labor markets,* which contain most of society's better-paying jobs. These primary labor markets tend to offer relatively good working conditions and compensation levels. Most of the jobs—even for blue-collar workers—within this primary sector pay wages significantly higher than minimum wage rates. In contrast, there are *secondary labor markets*, in which the working poor are most often confined. These secondary markets operate in a far different fashion from the primary labor market. Discrimination, very low wages, job instability, and little chance for improving one's conditions are cited as the main characteristics of secondary markets.[14] Minimum wages can provide some protection for workers employed within these sectors.

Future Trends

In line with the prophets of cybernetics and the disappearance of work, it might be anticipated that the problems of the working poor will diminish over time as our economy produces even more technological innovations and the requirements for marginal and menial labor diminish. Regrettably, however, the predictions are not based on fact.

First, what may be good for society in the long run might be a personal tragedy to an individual worker whose job is made redundant as a result of technological innovation and replaced by an advanced capital-intensive production process. Society's welfare in the aggregate might be improved in the long run by such changes (usually considered "progress"), but this process causes major problems for individual workers. Structural labor market problems, beyond cyclical unemployment, can be intensified by technological advancement.

Second, it is far from clear that the American economy's demand for low-wage labor is going to diminish in the near future. In fact, projections show that demand for marginal and menial labor should be increasing in the coming years—despite technological innovations.

When an economy grows, it does not just become larger; it change in several very important ways as part of the development process. The stages of growth in the United States, much as in other highly industrialized nations, have followed a general broad outline or path. At first the United States was mostly an agricultural nation with a very small manufacturing sector. The industrial revolution made manufacturing and subsidiary industries predominant, while the percentage of the labor force devoted to agriculture declined. The next step in the economic development of the United States has been the expansion of the service industries, which have been growing at a faster rate than the rest of the economy.[15]

Many expanding economic sectors employ large concentrations of marginal and menial labor; the health care industry is a prime example. Since World War II Americans, both as private consumers and through government spending, have allocated an ever larger percentage of their income gains for health care. In the language of economics, health care spending has had a relatively high income *elasticity*, or response to increased income. If Americans spend a greater percentage of their income on health care, then the percentage of employment accounted for by the health care sector also will tend to increase. The employment growth rate by this service sector, hence, will be larger than for the economy as a whole.

For example, the number of hospital attendants who are at the lower end of the occupational hierarchy and wage structure, has approximately doubled in each decade since 1940. If the projections of the Bureau of Labor Statistics prove to be correct, employment for hospital attendants will continue to increase at more than twice the projected growth rate for total employment under full employment conditions.[16] Other occupations that have a high percentage of low-wage workers will also be showing major employment gains—including teaching aides, child care workers, and various types of attendants.

This condition explains the seeming paradox of technological progress and a higher standard of living in coexistence with a continued need for low-wage labor. As an example, one study divided the labor force into five occupational and status groups and made employment supply projections for each segment through 1985. If these estimates are about right, then there will be a potential surplus of available workers in the so-called high wage Group I occupations as a result of a 66-percent growth in supply but only a 51-percent growth in projected employment. However, at the other end of the occupational status and wage structure the growth in requirements for low-wage Group IV (which includes such jobs as waiters and shipping clerks) and Group V (which includes such positions as kitchen workers and janitors) labor is expected to exceed the potential increase in available workers by about 6 percent and 3 percent respectively.[17]

Women have accounted for three out of every five additions to the labor force during the past 15 years. In 1977 the labor force increased by 2.6 million people, and this addition included over 1.5 million women and 143,000 teenagers. Women and youths make up a major portion of low-wage workers. Despite the future growth in average real per capita income and major advances in technology and production, it appears that the problems of low-wage workers are not going to cease in the coming years even as the American economy continues its economic development process.

Benefits and Costs of Minimum Wages

Granted that the working poor constitute a disturbingly large chunk of the American population in poverty, it does not necessarily follow that boosting the minimum wage is the appropriate cure for the ailment. Most of the critics of the minimum wage have concentrated on pointing out its ill effects, real or imaginary; but they have rarely proposed other ways to aid the working poor. However, several recent minimum wage critics have argued that, although a concerted effort in helping the working poor is justified, the wrong means are being used to achieve this end. Some analysts have argued that the costs produced by a wage floor far outweigh the benefits.

These arguments attempt to reduce the minimum wage controversy to a series of empirical questions. The reasoning rests on the presumption that if the benefits are greater than the costs, then the action should be undertaken—but that if the cost is larger than the derived benefit, then the proposed action should be rejected. This approach may be superficially appealing, but efforts to determine the real total costs and benefits of social programs frequently turn out to be disguises of normative judgments.

In the final analysis decisions concerning the minimum wage can not be left to a computer printout. However, it would be equally inappropriate to make decisions that affect millions of Americans and redound upon the entire economy without some attempt at quantiative analysis. We should ask ourselves—without rushing out to a computer—what types of benefits and costs do we expect minimum wages to generate? Even when researchers have disagreed about the specific magnitudes of the results, they have often agreed on the types of benefits and costs that will be produced.

Benefits

The first obvious benefit to be produced by the minimum wage is higher earnings for the working poor. The argument is that in the absence of minimum wages, the ranks of the working poor would be even larger. Higher wages for this segment of society will, in the words of the FLSA, reduce "labor conditions detrimental to the maintenance of the minimum standard of living necessary for health, efficiency, and general well-being of workers."

Minimum wages could also be viewed as a benefit in that they would alleviate the ill effects of discrimination and labor market pathologies. A wage floor could be a policy tool—but not the only one—used to counteract the negative impacts of dual or segmented labor markets.

Although the minimum wage is favored or opposed for numerous reasons, a major thrust of the FLSA is to moderate slightly the American economy's pattern of relative income distribution. For a society in which the top fifth of the population receives about six times as much income as the bottom fifth, a mild form of income redistribution in the guise of minimum wages could produce real benefits (Figure 7).

Also, for a society that still blesses the work ethic but also provides basic needs for the destitute, a decent minimum wage

24

could be a benefit in that it would provide the material incentives to induce more people to work rather than depend upon welfare. A decent minimum wage might also induce employers to improve investments in education, training, and other human capital outlays, which would result in increased productivity of the work force.

Figure 7. More than 14 percent of American families and 54 percent of households of unrelated individuals had annual incomes of less than $6,000 (1976).

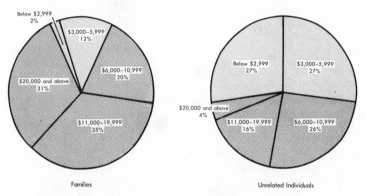

Families   Unrelated Individuals

Source: U.S. Department of Commerce, Bureau of the Census.

Workers are also consumers, and a higher level of compensation would allow more people to demand and consume an increasing quantity of goods and services. Additional consumption by workers would also provide more incentive for corporations to invest in plant, equipment, and human capital in an attempt to satisfy this higher level of demand. The coupled impact of increased demand for consumer and investment goods could help reduce unemployment as long as the economy is operating below conditions of full employment.

Arguments that increased minimum wages would lead to inflation place the poor in double jeopardy. Besides causing depriva-

25

tion, failure to increase minimum wages also makes the poor bear the brunt of the shrinking dollar and increasing prices. A lack of will to raise the minimum wage just to keep pace with inflation indicates a callousness concerning the lot of the poor.

Costs

There is another side to the coin: the minimum wage program does entail costs. Boosting the minimum wage raises the price of labor and reduces the demand for workers. Hence, a major cost of the minimum wage could be increased unemployment and job losses.

In addition to more unemployment, or a decline in job opportunities, a higher minimum wage gives a firm an added incentive to invest in capital-intensive and labor-saving production methods, which in turn could reduce the total demand for labor by substituting capital for labor. It is also argued that the minimum wage, besides increasing unemployment, adds fuel to the fires of inflation and boosts prices. The assumption here is that the working poor should be imbued with public spirit and be willing to place the common good above their needs. Increased minimum wages could also boost the prices of American export goods, and this would hurt the United States in international trade and finance.

Besides unemployment, inflation, and balance-of-payments problems, critics have also questioned the income redistribution impact of minimum wages on several grounds. First, many low-wage workers are part of a family group that has a total income above the median line. Second, it has been suggested that if income redistribution is a national goal, then it should be conducted directly by income and wage subsidies programs, as well as other social welfare measures.

An added cost sometimes cited is the impact minimum wages have on the wage structure of the entire economy. An increased minimum wage decreases the wage differential between high-paid workers and low-wage labor. Well-paid workers will seek to regain their old wage differential, which will generate a new round of wage hikes, a process referred to as cost-push inflation. Also, some analysts believe there are "natural" wage differentials between diffent regions of the country and even sections within a region. Minimum wages distort the differentials that would be the result of market forces; such distortion can hurt a region or an area, according to these arguments.

Minimum Wages and Social Welfare

The minimum wage in recent years has also taken on a further role. It is becoming more intimately linked with many government policies and proposed reforms. Not only is the minimum wage viewed by many as a tool that can influence the private sector of the economy, but increasingly it is also being used as a standard by which to establish government social welfare policies. For example, the Carter administration proposed the creation of public service jobs paying the minimum wage as an alternative to welfare. The use of the minimum wage as a policy indicator increases its importance as welfare reform becomes tied to the FLSA.

All too often public policymakers, analysts, and the media have become fixed on only one very limited aspect of the minimum wage. A highly distorted picture can be painted by focusing exclusively on either costs or benefits. It is easy to see that the minimum wage produces employment effects and income changes; but it also produces a lot more. It is much harder to look at the total picture—both the good and the bad. But that is no reason for avoiding a comprehensive assessment of the total impact of minimum wages.

Minimum wages are often compared to some ideal system, and on this basis the minimum wage often is judged to be a failure. Clearly, this is a misleading ground for comparison. Any meaningful evaluation of minimum wages must ask the question, What are the realistic economic, social, and political alternatives? The minimum wage is hardly a blueprint for the best of all worlds; yet it has become an effective policy tool in dealing with the plight of the working poor.

2

A Continuing Controversy

The Good Old Days

Despite the controversial history surrounding the minimum wage, the regulation of wages is nothing new. In fact, compensation for labor has been regulated throughout most of history—by either custom or law. Before 1800 wage regulation was used primarily to keep persons in their established economic place. For example, after the Black Death of 1348 the state did not allow the laborers who survived the plague to take advantage of their new-found bargaining strength. Wage assessment policies and regulations were key features during the Tudor period as well. Even before the American Revolution several American colonies had established wage regulations, either by establishing wage scales or by fixing maximum wages.[1]

With the rise of modern capitalism, wage regulations diminished. Thanks to a vast frontier and a labor demand that tended to exceed the supply, the American economy supported a relatively high general wage scale. It is estimated that during this early period the American wage rate for most positions ranged from 30 to as much as 300 percent higher than for the same jobs in England.[2]

But industrialization brought a new series of problems. The establishment of national markets meant that employment and the wages paid to labor were highly dependent upon the vagaries of new economic forces. This unpredictable invisible hand could decimate as well as uplift. Also, a factory system depersonalized the relationship between an employer and his numerous workers. Industrialization often reduced the skill level and the social status of labor. A growing number of workers were required to leave the land, work in the manufacturing sector, and live in rapidly expanding urban centers.

An increasing gross national product was one result of this economic and social transformation. But a growing urban poor, in the grip of what was called the "sweated labor" system, was also a by-product of these changes. Samuel Johnson once remarked, "A decent provision for the poor is the true test of civilization." During the early 1900s a growing number of leaders in the Progressive movement asserted that America was failing this test or at best had registered an incomplete. As a result of the efforts of these reformers, the plight of the working poor became known to the general public. The nation was moved by Monsignor John A. Ryan's book, *A Living Wage*, which appeared in 1906 and focused attention on low-wage labor. The same was true of Charles Spahr's *Essay on the Present Distribution of Wealth* and of numerous muckraking articles in periodicals.[3]

A "social gospel" was taken up by several religious leaders who saw the abuses of industrialization as a sharp contradiction with moral teachings, and the first American minimum wage campaigns took on elements of a religious revival. By 1907 annual immigration to the United States had reached more than 1 million persons per year, and this placed a strong downward pressure on wages for low-skill jobs. Social settlements were established in many of the most distressed districts in major American cities. Social workers and reformers gained a firsthand knowledge of the problems of the working poor. Many Americans increasingly saw the plight of low-paid labor as a kind of industrial jail.[4]

Liberal scholars also launched some of the first statistical research on wages in order to formulate minimum wage policy. The statistical method employed by most researchers at the time was to design a basic budget adequate to provide an urban single woman or married man with a wife and several children a "simple decency and working efficiency . . . and proper support."[5] Of course, this type of basic budget cannot be divorced from value judgments.

Until World War I state minimum wage boards tended to set the basic minimum level for a single woman at about $8 a week (or about $48 in 1978 dollars) and about $15 a week for a man with a wife and three children (about $89 a week in 1978 dollars). A 1912 study of women's wages found that 75 percent of female wage earners made less than this amount; 50 percent of the women workers were paid wages that produced an income equal to only three-fourths of the basic budget, and about 15 percent received wages that did not produce an income equal to even half of this level. A 1913-14 New York survey of factory payrolls found that about half the married men sampled earned less than this basic budget.[6]

Foreign Models

Typical of the trend in most American social or welfare legislation, the United States was a follower and not the leading nation in the field of minimum wages. Several labor economists, including J. R. Commons, and many state legislatures based American minimum wage plans in part on foreign models.

Industrialization in Australia produced a concentration of urban working poor similar to that in America. The province of Victoria, in reaction to antisweatshop campaigns, passed a minimum wage law in 1896 designed to cover six especially low-wage trades. A board was established for each of these industries representing employers, workers, and the general public, and the boards were given the power to establish fair and living wages for their respective industries. However, unlike the first laws passed by American state legislatures, the Australian laws covered both men and women workers. Other Australian provinces and New Zealand followed Victoria's example.

English reformers, and even several British establishment economists, examined with interest the experiments by former colonies. Not all English economists at the time totally rejected minimum wages. Even the great English neoclassical economist Alfred Marshall noted:

> The proposal that a minimum wage should be fixed by the authority of Government below which no man may work, and another below which no woman may work, has claimed the attention of students for a long while. If it could be made effective, its benefits would be so great that it might gladly be accepted, in spite of the fear that it would lead to malingering and some other abuses.[7]

In 1909 the United Kingdom established a minimum wage system. The Board of Trade was mandated to create wage boards for sweated industries subject to ratification by Parliament. Many of the early American state wage boards were modeled on the English systems. Employers, labor leaders, and public representatives formulated budgets that they considered basic or just above subsistence. Then the wage that would produce the income to cover a compromise budget was determined.

These basic budgets frequently were based on guesswork instead of statistical data on actual expenditure patterns. Often these wage board budgets simply expressed what a particular group regarded as necessary to achieve certain ends.[8]

Early State Laws

The pre–World War I drives for minimum wages in America in most cases were led by reformers outside the labor movement. Organized labor was mostly either apathetic or downright hostile to minimum wages. Many labor leaders feared that statutory minimum wage rates would turn into maximum wages. Also, given the social climate of the period, organized labor was properly concerned that government would side with business interests if political authorities were given the power to establish wage rates.

In line with the American Federation of Labor's craft union orientation, a skilled worker could understandably prefer the winning of collective bargaining rights as far more important than minimum wage legislation. Only after institutional arrangements had been legalized on a federal level could unions afford to direct their real energies in favor of minimum wages.

State minimum wage laws covered only female workers and minors, in line with a 1908 Supreme Court decision (*Muller* v. *Oregon*) in which a maximum hour regulation covering women and minors was upheld because of their "special condition."[9] The Oregon law only regulated hours and did not deal with wages.

In 1912 Massachusetts passed the first state minimum wage law. The National Consumers League—a group of middle-class reformers—was the prime lobbying force in favor of the legislation. The law provided for minimum wage boards that could determine "living wage" levels for selected industries, taking into consideration employer production costs. Although these levels were nonmandatory, the state could publish the names of firms that paid less than the levels established by a wage board.

In 1912 the Progressive Party called for national minimum wages for women and minors. Opponents objected on two main grounds: (1) minimum wage laws would violate the individual's right to contract, which was viewed as a basic wellspring of liberty, and (2) a minimum wage could hurt the very people it was designed to help, since higher wages would lead to more unemployed workers. Harvard University, interestingly enough, went to considerable pains to prove the second point. The pay of the scrubwomen in its Widener Library would have been 2 cents an hour higher under the state-suggested level. Rather than pay the added 2 cents an hour or have its name printed in the newspapers as an employer who paid less than the suggested minimum, Harvard "resolved" the problem by replacing the twenty scrub-women with male workers, whose wages were not subject to the regulation.

Although the Progressive Party was soundly defeated in 1912, its platform had some effect, and fifteen states passed minimum wage laws in the following decade. Most of the state laws adopted the English system—except that only women and minors were covered—and they sought to establish boards for low-wage industries. Only the Utah law contained a specific wage level written into its bill.[10]

Minnesota's experience is illustrative of the situation faced by the states that passed minimum wage legislation. To rephrase T. S. Eliot: Between passing a law and enforcing a specific regulation falls the shadow. The 1913 Minnesota legislation contained no flat rates written into the law, and industry wage boards were to establish minimum wages. In state after state, lawsuits were filed by employers in an effort to gain state court injunctions blocking any wage regulations. Many state wage boards faced legal battles for years before any regulations were issued—let alone enforced. Minnesota issued its first minimum wage order in 1914. However, an employer's group won a state court injunction. The state supreme court upheld the constitutionality of the 1913 law, but it was not until 1918 that the first minimum wage regulations were issued by Minnesota state authorities, and even these were not vigorously enforced.

California and Wisconsin minimum wage commissions delayed actions pending a United States Supreme Court ruling on state regulations of minimum wages. In one of the longest games of "wait and see," the citizens of Ohio voted in the 1912 election to adopt a state minimum wage regulation; however, it was not until 1933 that the Ohio legislature got around to passing such legislation.

The first United States Supreme Court test of state minimum wage legislation resulted from the attempted enforcement of the

1913 Oregon state minimum wage law, in the case of *Stettler* v. *O'Hara*. The Oregon Supreme Court had upheld the police powers of the state to regulate minimum wages, noting that excessively low wages injured public health, morals, and welfare. The state supreme court decision was grounded in large measure on a brief written by Louis D. Brandeis and filed by the state. Once on the U.S. Supreme Court, Brandeis disqualified himself from voting on the case. The high court divided four to four on the case, sustaining the state supreme court's decision. No written decision was issued, and so *Stettler* v. *O'Hara* left many questions unanswered.

At the time of World War I the minimum wage movement was skating on thin ice. A majority of states passed only weak laws or had regulators who did not—or could not—enforce their regulations; the U.S. Supreme Court was divided and had issued no written opinion on the issue and, most important, the reformist movement appeared to have lost some of its steam and its support by the public. Whatever impact the basic budgets might have had was diluted by inflation as most state boards failed to boost their cost of living budgets.[11] Writing during this period, Walter Lippmann saw the system of state minimum wage boards as producing "not a wage so . . . women can live well, not enough to make life rich and a welcome experience, but just enough to secure existence amid drudgery in gray boarding houses and cheap restaurants."[12]

In 1923 the U.S. Supreme Court received a second opportunity to review state minimum wage legislation in *Adkins* v. *Children's Hospital*. Willy Adkins was an elevator operator employed by Children's Hospital in the District of Columbia. The Court found five to three that the minimum wage regulations violated the fifth and fourteenth amendments to the Constitution. This case cast a pall over state minimum wage legislation. Since his daughter served on the District's wage board, Justice Brandeis once again disqualified himself from the case. Justice George Sutherland wrote the court's decision, which many historians have viewed as one of the "all-time peaks of Supreme Court conservatism."[13] Sutherland's majority opinion concluded:

There are limits to power, and when these have been passed, it becomes the plain duty of the courts in the proper exercise of their authority to so declare. To sustain the individual freedom of action contemplated by the Constitution is not to strike down the common good but to exalt it; for surely the good of society as a whole cannot be better served than by the preservation against arbitrary restraint of the liberties of its constituent members.[14]

Two dissents were written in the case. Chief Justice William Taft argued that the "employees . . . are not on a full level of equality with their employer and in their necessitous circumstances are prone to accept pretty much anything that is offered."[15] Taft said that there was no absolute freedom to contract, and he insisted that it was not the function of the court to hold congressional acts invalid simply because they contained economic views that the court believed to be unwise or unsound. Justice Oliver Wendell Holmes, in his dissenting opinion, agreed with these points made by Taft and added that the Constitution was not married to any social thinker, be it Adam Smith or Herbert Spencer. The law, Holmes stated, did not compel anybody to pay anything, and there are certain legal and fair standards any contract must meet if it is to have the sanction of law.

After 1923 six other minimum wage laws were declared unconstitutional on the basis of this decision. Only the Massachusetts nonmandatory law was upheld, in *Commonwealth* v. *Boston Transcript Co.* (1924). But the high court found it unconstitutional for the state to publish in the newspapers the names of firms not paying the established minimum wage. This nullified the only real power given to the state boards.

By 1930 the box score for minimum wage laws was—seventeen state laws originally enacted; three of them repealed; seven found unconstitutional; and one (Wisconsin) amended. The remaining state wage boards experienced difficulties in enforcing their regulations. Their concern was that if they pressed too hard they would be taken to court, and the result would be that they in all probability would have to close up their regulatory shop. Funds to carry out their work tended to be quite small. Wisconsin changed its law to require that the wages paid to women and minors not be oppressive, instead of calling for establishment of a living wage.

It is important to note that early supporters of the minimum wage sought only to curb the worst abuses. To the charge that they were against free markets and competition, the minimum wage defenders responded that their objective was to raise the plane of competition—not to end it.

The New Deal

The prospect of minimum wages changed drastically as a result of the Great Depression. The goal was to move the economy by boosting aggregate demand. The early New Deal game plan was embodied in the National Industrial Recovery Act (NRA). In essence, the NRA was an attempt to solve the problems caused by the depression through a system of government-underwritten price and wage codes. It was hoped that the codes would block further increases in unemployment and cut down the number of workers forced into idleness. The NRA became law in June 1933, and through a suspension of antitrust laws it tried to bolster private enterprise with the cooperation of government, business, and labor.

In 1931 the Chamber of Commerce of the United States had endorsed a system that had many of the features of the NRA, including "the philosophy of a planned economy."[16] To win labor cooperation, Section 7(a) of the act guaranteed employees the right to organize and bargain collectively. Employers would comply with maximum hours of labor, minimum rates of pay, and other conditions of employment approved or prescribed by the president.[17]

Business interests were in far better shape to use NRA to their advantage than either labor or government. Many of the NRA

37

codes of fair competition were drafted by business trade associations or industry executives. Before it was killed by the Supreme Court, the NRA approved 557 basic codes, the labor provisions of 19 joint NRA-AAA (Agricultural Adjustment Administration) codes, and 189 supplementary codes. Labor members participated in the administration of only 37 of these codes, and labor members did not always have the right to vote.

About 55 percent of all workers covered by NRA labor standard codes (or 338 codes) had a basic minimum of 40 cents or more (about $2.00 in 1978 dollars); 14 codes, covering 5 percent of all employees, provided for a basic minimum wage of less than 30 cents an hour (or about $1.50 in 1978 dollars).[18] Where industry and labor clashed over NRA codes, industry won in every case.[19] The deterioration of wages in some sectors of the economy during the depression led several labor officials to pay more attention to the role of minimum wages. In 1935 the Supreme Court found the NRA to be unconstitutional (*United States* v. *A.L.A. Schechter*). With this decision the NRA wage codes lost the force of law.

Meanwhile seven states had passed "new design" minimum wage laws in 1933. The New York state law required a minimum wage for women to be fairly and reasonably commensurate with the value of the service or class of service rendered. The case of *Morehead* v. *New York ex rel. Tipaldo* (1936) arose out of a violation of the New York "new design" law. By a vote of five to four the court found the New York law was similar to the issues involved in the *Adkins* case, and hence the Empire State's law was equally unconstitutional. In the majority decision Justice Pierce Butler found that the New York law was no different from the old District of Columbia regulation and that both laws were contrary to the due process clause of the Fourteenth Amendment.

Just when it seemed that all minimum wage laws were unconstitutional, the high court once again reopened the issue in *West Coast Hotel Company* v. *Parrish* (1937). In a complete reversal the court upheld by a vote of five to four the constitutionality of a

Washington state minimum wage law. In the majority decision Chief Justice Charles Evans Hughes argued,

> The Constitution does not speak of freedom of contract. It speaks of liberty and prohibits the deprivation of liberty without due process of law. In prohibiting that deprivation the Constitution does not recognize an absolute and uncontrollable liberty. . . . But the liberty safeguarded is liberty in a social organization which requires the protection of law against the evils which menace the health, safety, morals and welfare of the people. Liberty under the Constitution is thus necessarily subject to the restraints of due process, and regulation which is reasonable in relation to its subject and is adopted in the interests of the community is due process. . . .
>
> We think that the . . . decision in the Adkins case was a departure from the true applications of the principles governing the regulation by the State of the relation of employer and employed.[20]

What can explain the Supreme Court's change? Critics have charged that the court, rather than experiencing a change of heart, was motivated by a desire to save its own skin. According to this view the court was under intense pressure from the White House and other pro–New Deal forces. The battle heightened with attempts to pack the court. As one historian put it: "A switch in time saved nine."[21] The 1936 and 1937 cases involved the same court members. All it took to reverse the court's decision was the change of one vote, and Justice Owen Roberts made the difference, although a technical point was also involved. In the 1936 case even the lawyers for the state did not question the *Adkins* decision. All they argued was that the New York state law was different from the old District of Columbia regulation. On this point Justice Roberts could not agree, for he felt that the two laws were quite similar. This was all the court was asked to rule on. But the 1937 case went to the root of the issue and questioned the basic *Adkins* decision, and Justice Roberts did not believe the *Adkins* decision to be correct.

Lasting Federal Legislation

Two major federal acts regulating wages predate the federal Fair Labor Standards Act: The Walsh-Healey Public Contracts Act of 1936 and the Davis-Bacon Act of 1931. These earlier laws were made possible by pre-1937 court decisions that the government could regulate wages for work performed under its contracts. The Walsh-Healey Act provides the setting of minimum wages on certain federal contracts that involve at least $10,000, and the minimum wage—unlike the FLSA system—is to be based upon prevailing community rates. The act also sets time-and-one-half premium pay rates for daily hours in excess of eight. The Davis-Bacon Act sets wage and hour standards for federally funded construction work.

Also, in *National Labor Relations Board* v. *Jones & Laughlin Steel Corporation* (1937), the Supreme Court adopted the doctrine that when an industry draws a substantial part of its raw materials or sends a substantial part of its finished product through the channels of interstate commerce, any activity that interrupts production affects interstate commerce. Hence, these so-called indirect activities may be regulated by Congress under the interstate commerce power of the Constitution. In the past the court had found that such operations as production were not interstate commerce and could not be regulated by Congress. This case in addition to the *West Coast Hotel* case opened the way for federal action on minimum wage legislation.

The FLSA

With strong Roosevelt administration leadership, a Federal Fair Labor Standards bill was introduced in Congress in May 1937. The bill provided for a minimum wage and a maximum work week to be stated in the statute but to be applied industry by industry under a five-member board that was to administer the act. In addition to conservative lawmakers and business groups who were

40

against the proposal, organized labor was divided on the merits of the bill. American Federation of Labor leaders were still concerned about the impact of federal regulation of wages, and they still felt that minimum wage legislation might hamper collective bargaining efforts. As a result, A.F. of L. president William Green took a highly equivocal position on the bill.[22]

The labor federation offered six amendments to the bill and made its support of the bill conditional upon the acceptance of these changes. The amendments were designed to safeguard collective bargaining and to limit the scope of government regulation over wages. The Congress of Industrial Organizations opposed the wage board system and proposed that the bill mandate a flat minimum wage of 40 cents an hour and a 35-hour maximum work week. Ignoring labor's reservations, President Roosevelt called a special session of Congress to act on the bill in November 1937. Congress responded slowly and passed a much-amended minimum wage law nine months later.

The 1938 law set the minimum wage at 25 cents per hour, to rise gradually to 40 cents by 1945. As a result of inflationary pressures from World War II and sustained tight labor markets, a virtually universal minimum of 40 cents was achieved by 1944, more than one year before the statutory 40-cents minimum would have taken effect. Employers were required to pay one-and-one-half times the worker's regular wage rate for any hours worked in excess of 40 per week. So many exemptions had been written into the bill that at one point during the congressional debate Martin Dies filed a satirical amendment calling on the Labor Department to report back to Congress within 90 days after the bill's passage on whether any worker was covered by the act. Only about one out of four workers was covered by the original 1938 FLSA. Of this number, roughly 300,000 received wage increases when the law went into effect at 25 cents an hour. Two years later 650,000 workers received a wage boost when the 30-cent minimum wage went into effect.[23]

The administrator of the Wage and Hour Division of the Labor Department was given the power to appoint labor, business, and public representatives to industry committees that could, within established limits, recommend rates different from the legislated minimums. The industry-by-industry committee system turned out to be ineffective. The industry committee system was designed to allow fine-tuning of wage contracts, but in practice it proved an obstacle to action.[24]

On the basis of this experience, Congress in 1949 abolished the industry committee system and replaced it with a single minimum rate. An exception to the flat-rate system applied to Puerto Rico, the Virgin Islands, and American Samoa. Because wages had been historically lower in these islands, industry committees were authorized to set rates lower than mainland minimums. The Supreme Court upheld the constitutionality of the FLSA in a 1941 case (*United States* v. *F. W. Darby Lumber Company*).

FLSA Amendments

There have been six major amendments to the FLSA since 1938. Periodic amendments have raised the level of the minimum wage, and coverage has been greatly expanded. However, the overtime pay formula of one-and-one-half times the basic wage rate for more than 40 hours per week has remained unchanged.

During the first four decades after passage of the FLSA, Congress boosted the hourly minimum wage from the initial 25 cents to $2.65. The more than tenfold rise reflected inflation and growth in productivity. Since the wages of low-paid workers tend to cluster near the minimum wage, each time the floor is raised many workers receive wage boosts (Figure 8). Beyond the direct impact, the minimum wage can indirectly raise the wages paid to workers who earn slightly more than the floor. One method of analysis of the level of minimum wage is to examine the wage floor as a percentage of the average wage paid in the manufacturing sector (Figure 9). From 1950 to 1977 the minimum wage has ranged from 40 percent to 53 percent of the average paid in the manufacturing sector.

Figure 8.   Many low-paid workers receive wage increases when the minimum wage is raised.

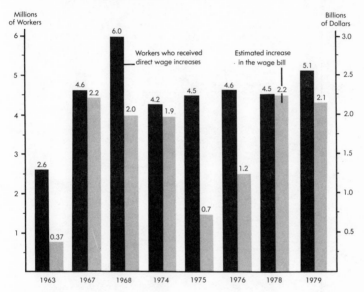

Source: U.S. Department of Labor.

The minimum wage as a percentage of the average wage in the manufacturing sector shows a clear pattern. The proportion reaches a relative high point after congressional amendments to the FLSA are passed. But then this percentage figure falls as inflationary forces and wage gains in the manufacturing sector eat away at the protection provided by minimum wages. For this reason it has been suggested that minimum wages be indexed to a proportion of the manufacturing wage. Congress would no longer have to pass amendments to the FLSA to increase the minimum wage, since it would automatically increase in line with inflation.

Figure 9. The protection offered by the minimum wage has trailed inflation and productivity between congressional rounds.

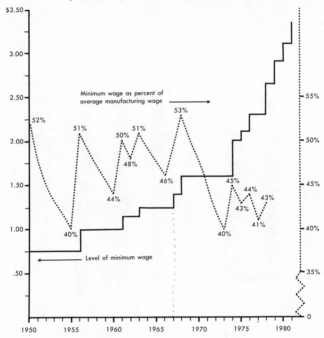

Source: U.S. Department of Labor.

As noted, initially the minimum wage law extended protection only to a minority of workers and denied coverage to employees in several major low-wage industries. Since 1961 Congress has repeatedly extended the coverage of the FLSA (Figure 10). The FLSA was amended in 1963 to prohibit discrimination in wages of

Figure 10. Minimum wage coverage for nonsupervisory workers has steadily expanded.

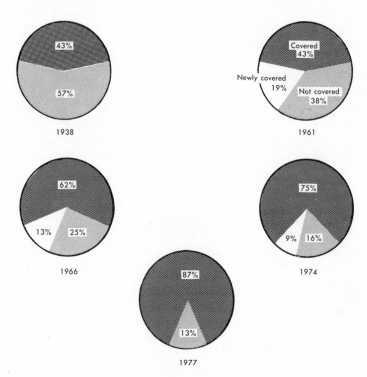

Source: U.S. Department of Labor.

covered employees due to sex. As part of President Johnson's anti-poverty efforts, coverage was vastly increased in 1966 to protect workers in several major low-wage industries, including laundries, restaurants, hotels, farms, hospitals, and nursing homes. For many of the newly covered workers, Congress passed a temporary lower minimum wage level to ease the transition period for firms in these industries. There still are groups that remain outside the pale of

45

FLSA, including some who may need the protection most. Small farms and small retail and service enterprises, as well as many state and local public employers, are not covered by FLSA. Some workers are protected by state laws. But before the 1977 amendments to the FLSA only five states and the District of Columbia had established minimum wage rates above the federal level.[25] As in many other areas, reliance on social legislation has shifted from state legislatures to the federal Congress.

An important feature of the FLSA is a realization that some workers may require special exemptions from the minimum wage level. Section 14 of the act establishes a certification procedure that can be used for full-time students, learners in industries other than retail or service, and handicapped workers employed in sheltered workshops. For example, under the law it is possible for employers to secure certification from the Department of Labor for the employment of full-time students (employed up to 20 hours a week or full time during vacation periods) at 85 percent of the federal minimum wage. In the year ending June 1977 the department granted about 575,000 exemptions for workers to be employed at the lower wage rate. However, many of these granted exemptions were not utilized by employers. In most cases an employer can hire a student and pay the lower wage level without waiting for a reply from the Department of Labor. Forms must be filed, but in general the procedure is pro forma.

Administration

In the large and open U.S. economy, it takes more than Congress passing a law to make the minimum wage a reality. Some employers, seeing the prospects of higher profits, might not comply and might pay workers a wage lower than the legal minimum. It cannot be assumed that all workers will know the legal protection afforded them under the FLSA. Even if a worker knows about the protection offered by the minimum wage, the individual may feel—

for various reasons—that a complaint would be futile and might result in the loss of a job. Some workers—particularly undocumented aliens, whose numbers have increased in recent years—may be working at below the minimum wage and are not in a position to blow the whistle on their employers.

The Wage and Hour Division of the Labor Department is responsible for enforcement of the FLSA. Because of resource constraints, the division initiates few actions to ensure compliance, and its enforcement activities consist of responding to complaints. During fiscal 1977 the division received about 49,000 complaints alleging violations of the FLSA. Almost 90 percent of the division's investigation time is spent looking into these allegations. The number of complaints filed with the division follows a general pattern, peaking after a round of congressional amendments to the FLSA. In fiscal 1977 enforcement activity found that 371,000 workers experienced minimum wage underpayments for an aggregate annual sum of $37 million. A total of some $20 million in unpaid minimum wages was restored to 266,000 workers.[26]

The fact that $17 million worth of alleged minimum wage underpayments was not restored to 105,000 workers was due to enforcement problems. Before going to court an effort is made to have employers pay the statutory wages. However, because of the number of complaints involved, the Labor Department is selective in its use of litigation. The goal is to establish legal precedents in situations where voluntary compliance fails. In fiscal 1977 the Labor Department filed almost 2,500 court suits alleging violations of the FLSA, and roughly $9 million was restored to 47,000 workers as a result of legal action.

A prime example of the types of cases the Labor Department takes to court involves exemption questions. Some employers will claim that they are not covered by the law. For example, in 1977 a federal court of appeals rejected an employer's claim, in *Brennan* v. *Western Union Telegraph*, that executive, professional, and administrative employees who performed other work during a strike retained their exempt status under FLSA. In another case a federal court ruled that an employer must pay waiters and waitresses at least half of the minimum wage regardless of the total tips the workers receive (*Richard* v. *Marriott,* 1977).

But the figures listed above do not represent total noncompliance with the FLSA. Although the Wage and Hour Division has statistics on the number of complaints filed and the resulting actions, these figures do not include situations in which an employer pays less than the minimum wage and no complaint is filed or investigation launched. The incidence of unreported compliance, obviously, can not be measured. Attempts to speculate about the seriousness of the problem are of a kind with guesses about cheating on income tax returns, or guessing the number of undocumented aliens in the country, or estimating the size of the subterranean economy.

Although analysts cannot directly estimate with a fine degree of precision the degree of noncompliance to the minimum wage, there are indications that violations of the law are a serious problem. The federal government's Current Population Survey (CPS) collects information on hourly earnings. Statistics for May 1975 disclosed the following data regarding workers earning less than the minimum wage:

	Number (thousands)	Percent of total employment
All workers	3,835	6.2
Teenagers	1,205	22.0
Adult males	850	2.6
Adult females	1,781	7.7

Assuming that the reporting is accurate, the explanation might be either that respondents were not covered by the minimum wage or that employers were in violation of the FLSA. Edward M.

Gramlich reasoned that if noncompliance with the law was a major cause of people's being paid less than the wage floor, then the actual proportion of a class of workers earning less than the minimum wage should hardly differ between legally covered and uncovered industries once the data are adjusted for the different wage dstributions within industries. If incomplete coverage is the problem, then there should be large differences in these ratios. He found that the ratios were quite similar in several different industries. This is not direct proof, but it does indicate that noncompliance with the minimum wage is a serious problem.[27]

Gramlich considered only the two possible reasons listed above for why the ratios might be different. However, there are other factors that he did not consider, which might alter these results. Workers could be paid under the minimum because their employer had obtained a legal exemption, or they may be tipped employees who can be paid under the minimum. Despite these complications, it appears that the thrust of Gramlich's estimates is correct, and they indicate that noncompliance with the law is a real problem.

Research by Orley Ashenfelter and Robert Smith indicates that there is a great incentive to cheat on minimum wages and that many employers yield to the temptation. Their calculations show that if government enforcement of the law is random, then the expected benefits from noncompliance can outweigh the costs of possibly being caught.[28] However, government enforcement is not a random process. There were fewer than 1,500 compliance officers when this study was conducted, but they were not evenly assigned in different parts of the country. For example, according to Ashenfelter and Smith about 37 percent of covered employees paid less than the minimum wage were in the relatively low-wage southern part of the United States. But about half of all government compliance officers were assigned to work in the South in that year, which would indicate that government enforcement shows

49

some planning and is not just a random process. It may affect the extent of actual, as well as discovered, noncompliance.

The two analysts tried to measure compliance with the law using May 1973 CPS data on earnings. They defined compliance as the proportion of workers earning below the minimum wage before enactment of the law who earned at least the minimum wage or who lost their jobs in the covered sector of the economy after enactment. Using this definition they found the highest compliance rates in the South and in cases affecting women and nonwhites, and they estimated the following compliance rates for fully covered workers:

	Compliance rates for fully covered workers (percent)
South	78
Non-South	60
Male	57
Female	73
White	67
Nonwhite	79

Employers who operate in the South or who hire a large portion of women or nonwhite workers may have a greater economic incentive to violate the law. But this incentive may be more than offset by a higher possibility of being caught. Even with incomplete compliance, Ashenfelter and Smith found, the minimum wage still had the power to change wage structures—for example, between the covered and uncovered sectors of the economy.

There are problems associated with estimates based on data collected from the May CPS. Frequently the respondent may not know the specific earnings of all workers in the household. Also, the two researchers cautioned that their estimation techniques contained many assumptions and sources of bias that they could not directly measure. These figures should not be considered anything more than very rough estimates, and some of the specific estimates did not have the standard level of statistical significance. It appears that the issue of noncompliance with the law is a problem, and it will require improved enforcement methods if the congressional mandate is to be carried out.

Historical Conditions

The nation may worship at the shrine of the work ethic, but the historical record shows that many employers have tried to purchase this devotion at a very cheap price. A system of state laws appeared unworkable, and a federal system was required. In an analysis of the wage floor it is important to compare it with more than some abstract concept of perfect competition. More to the point is to compare the minimum wage with the actual historical conditions it replaced.

Both in the level of compensation and in coverage, the FLSA started out as a modest program. Despite expanded coverage and increases in the dollar figure, the wage floor still directly affects only people who tend to be on the bottom rung of the economic ladder. However, the indirect effects of the program have an impact on the rest of society. When the FLSA was passed during the Great Depression, its main role was to police labor market conditions in the private sector. Because of vast institutional and economic changes, the minimum wage's influence has grown in scope as the welfare state has matured.

3

The Impact of Minimum Wages

> I often say that when you can measure what you are speaking about, and express it in numbers, you know something about it; but when you cannot express it in numbers, your knowledge is of a meager and unsatisfactory kind; it may be the beginning of knowledge, but you have scarcely in your thoughts, advanced to the stage of a science, whatever the matter may be.
>
> —Lord Kelvin

A Matter of Faith and Facts

Many practitioners of the dismal science have asserted that economics has made the crucial quantitative leap envisioned by Lord Kelvin and has become "the queen of social sciences."[1] Armed with advanced statistical methods, an econometric arsenal, and complex computer models, George Stigler pronounced in his 1965 presidential address before the American Economic Association, "I am convinced that economics is finally at the threshold of its golden age—nay, we already have one foot through the door."[2] He stopped short of telling the multitudes what awaited them on the inside. Apparently presidents of learned societies are no less prone to rhetoric than other politicians.

If Stigler was right, then it would appear to be an easy matter to discover the quantitative impact of minimum wages. Economists have aimed their bulging arsenal at an analysis of wage determination, and few areas of governmental economic policy have been subjected to more intense research. But controversy about the impact of minimum wages persists unabated, and economic investigation has offered little help. The vast majority of researchers still employ—in one form or another—the standard analytical tools, though embroidered with computer printouts, outlined by Alfred Marshall at the turn of the century. It is not uncommon in any science for people to hold different beliefs on the same subject before numerous experiments are conducted; but after repeated results and mounting data, one side usually admits that it is wrong. An alternative is that practitioners holding one set of beliefs grow old and die and are not replaced by new converts; this process has not taken place in the minimum wage arena.

The record of the economics profession in the 1970s hardly justifies the lofty claims and hopes of the numerologists. There is no question, however, that the growing use of computers and advanced statistical techniques has vastly shifted the profession's mode of operation. Casual empiricism has been replaced by touted rigorous quantitative analysis. The experience of the economics profession with the study of minimum wages is a good case study for reasssessing the claim of practitioners that the new technology has advanced the analytical powers of economists. Presumably the new tools should provide heretofore unrevealed insights into appraising the true impact of minimum wage legislation, including its effect on unemployment and, more important, its effect on the lot of the working poor.

Unlike the proverbial camel, economists have not made the anticipated progress; they may have their noses in the tent, but they are far from resting their bodies inside. The golden age in which the

53

quantitative findings of different researchers agree remains as elusive as ever, although more economists than at any other time are chasing new answers to age-old questions. A major tenet of the scientific method is that an experiment can be repeated by different researchers and the same results will be reproduced. In the area of minimum wages, economists have not even been able to agree on what constitutes a proper experiment. It is disconcerting how often one can guess the findings of a minimum wage study merely by knowing who is conducting it or paying for it. To make matters worse, even when analysts working the same side of the street can agree on the qualitative directions of minimum wage impacts, their specific estimates continue to vary significantly in magnitude. Given certain views or biases, the evaluators can marshal the "facts" to support their contentions.

A major percentage of the vast differences in quantitative findings is due to the highly diverse research methods, assumptions, definitions, and economic models used by different analysts. It is like the old story of the blind men investigating the elephant: the results and estimates often are determined by the assumptions that are made and the particular part of the broad problem that is being touched.

Our first task, then, should be to examine not only the findings but also the underlying assumptions made to reach the conclusions. Suppose one economist predicts that a 15-percent increase in the federal minimum wage will reduce employment by 150,000 jobs and will increase teenage unemployment by 4 percentage points. Meanwhile another analyst using the same computer concludes that the employment impact of the law would be negligible. Where do these numbers come from? Clearly, we should not only examine the quantitative findings, but we should also investigate the contributing methods used by different researchers to reach contradictory estimates.

Even the most advanced techniques are not immune to biased assumptions, and the acceptance of the conclusions still requires a large dose of faith, allowing outsiders an even larger measure of skepticism to question whether the faith is warranted. The analysis that follows is based on balanced doses of faith and skepticism.

Theory and Reason

Before the advent of the computer and econometrics, an economist's work was largely done once he spun an appropriate theory of how the economy functioned. The economist may have taken a casual look at what little data existed at the time, but the conclusions were largely based on sheer faith. The mode of analysis was highly Aristotelian, using deductive logic buttressed by only meager empirical observations. Even if the data existed, the technology to process the numbers for statistical testing was extremely crude by modern standards.

At first glance, there would seem to be no problem in measuring the impact of minimum wages. All an analyst would have to do is to calculate employment, unemployment, wages, income, and investment before the policy change in minimum wages and then repeat the same procedure sometime after the change. This method of before-and-after counting was the prime tool employed by the first minimum wage researchers, and it is still used in assessing the impact of the wage floor. Such studies have played a major role in continued minimum wage debates and are often cited in congressional deliberations as well as in the media.

There are several major problems with this method of investigation. First, the costs involved in obtaining comprehensive data can be prohibitive. To obviate the problem, researchers have followed two routes. They have either narrowed their field of investigation or derived sample estimates by using limited survey data. For example, instead of counting numerous variables in randomly sampled parts of the nation, some surveys were confined to only a few cities, industries, or labor market subgroups (such as teenagers). Whether what is discovered for a relatively small group can be extrapolated for the entire population is often, at best, an open question. The fact that minimum wages create disemployment—a loss of job opportunities—for teenagers in a selected southern-based industry does not necessarily mean that the same quantitative impact can be expected for all adult workers in the entire nation.

If survey samples are used to derive estimates, then there are numerous statistical reasons why an estimate may be biased and incorrect. To give just one example: many statistical estimates employ the method of a random sample allowing each member of a population an equal chance of being included in the sample's survey. It is not always an easy task to select a true random sample, and representative groups can be either overcounted or undercounted, which can create a biased estimate. In the real world the number of workers employed before and after a minimum wage increase is rarely known; the same is true for the other variables. But there is a second flaw with this method of just counting absolute before-and-after changes.

This type of analysis implicitly makes the *ceteris paribus*—all other things being equal—assumption. It assumes that during the one or two years under investigation nothing else besides the minimum wage has changed. This is hardly, if ever, the case, and reliance on this method of analysis can produce highly misleading conclusions. Suppose the economy experiences an economic boom after the boost in minimum wages, and employment rises even in industries affected by the minimum wage. On the basis of these data, many people may draw the conclusion that the minimum wage has not decreased employment—in fact it may have even helped increase the number of jobs. But if the economy plunges into a slump after the rise in the minimum wage, a conclusion that the minimum wage increase has created massive unemployment may be equally unfounded.

Most early minimum wage studies used the before-and-after absolute counting method, and as a result they suffered from this basic flaw. The major distinguishing feature between these early studies and more recent minimum wage investigations is that the latter have attempted to conduct statistical experiments that take into account the fact that other economic variables, besides the minimum wage, can and do change. If increased unemployment is discovered, then the more recent studies try to determine how much of the unemployment is attributable to minimum wages and how much is due to other factors, such as shifting business conditions or demographic changes. It should also be noted, however, that conducting statistical experiments is a highly complex task.

A Small Dose of Theory

One way to show the differences between the newer statistical research and the older absolute counting method is to consider what economists call a *demand curve* or *demand function* (Figure 11). Theory indicates an inverse relationship between wage rates and the number of employees or hours of labor hired by a firm. As the wage rate increases, the number of workers hired is reduced. This demand curve is pictured as D_0 in Figure 11. If all other variables are held constant, D_0 depicts the negative relationship between wages and the level of employment.

If the wage rate increased to W_0, then N_0 workers will be hired. Suppose the wage rate increased to W_1 because of a higher minimum wage. Then employment would be reduced to a lower level, N_3. This reduction in job opportunities, or job loss effect, due to minimum wages would be N_0 minus N_3. But suppose that at the same time the economic activity of the nation picked up. This would shift the demand curve out to the right, to D_1. At any given wage, employers would be willing to employ more workers. If the wage had not been increased and the wage rate had stayed at W_0, then employment would have been higher, at N_1. Instead the increased wage rate, W_1, coupled with the new demand curve, D_1, resulted in an employment level of N_2.

Figure 11. The demand curve shows the relationship between wage rates and the number of workers hired.

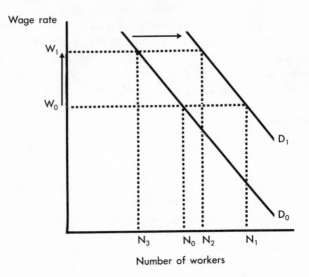

A counting of the absolute numbers before and after would show that prior to the new minimum wage employment was N_0, and even with the higher minimum wage employment grew to N_2. Many recent studies would interpret these results quite differently. One interpretation might be: if it were not for the increased minimum wage, employment would have grown to N_1 instead of the lower level of N_2. The negative impact of the minimum wage, or its job loss effect, then would be N_1 minus N_2.

By controlling for other variables, an analyst can find—at least in theory—what part of the total change in labor demand was due to the minimum wage and what percentage was caused by other forces. But demand is only half the picture; one must also consider supply. A supply curve might be expected to have a positive

Figure 12. Estimates of minimum wage unemployment impacts require examination of both supply and demand.

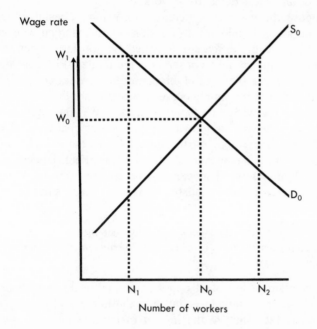

Number of workers

relationship to the wage rate. As wages increase, say within an industry, a greater number of workers would be willing to work in this sector. A supply curve coupled with a demand curve is shown in Figure 12.

By considering the demand and supply relationship, one can see that the loss of job opportunities is not exactly the same thing as unemployment. For example, suppose the wage rate is W_0, then the number of workers employed is N_0. To use the language of economists, the labor market is in equilibrium; at the given market

59

wage rate the number of workers demanded equals the number of workers wishing to supply their labor. There is neither unemployment nor an excess demand for workers.

Suppose the wage rate increases to W_1 as a result of the minimum wage. Employment falls along the demand curve from N_0 to N_1, and the difference is called the job loss effect. To estimate this impact, all an observer is required to do is consider the demand curve. The loss of job opportunities does not require any estimation of the supply curve. But that is not the end of the story. Since the wage rate has increased to W_1, the number of workers seeking work has grown to N_2, because higher wages tend to attract additional labor into the market. Under these conditions, unemployment is larger than just the job loss effect. Unemployment is N_2 minus N_1. This can also be seen by considering the definitions used in labor statistics. The labor force is defined as follows:

Labor force = the number employed + number unemployed (For this definition, unemployment is defined as: Unemployment = labor force − number employed)

To estimate the loss of job opportunities, or the disemployment impact, it is necessary to count only the number of employed workers. But to analyze the impact of minimum wages upon unemployment, it is necessary to consider not only the number employed, but also the changes in the labor force. This explains the greater complexity in estimating the unemployment impact of the minimum wage than in gauging the loss of job opportunities.

The slopes of the demand and supply curves can indicate the size of these minimum wage effects. If the curves are very flat—say, close to horizontal—then the quantity of labor demanded and supplied will be highly responsive to the wage. A small change in the wage rate will produce very big changes in the demand and supply of labor. But if the curves have very steep slopes—say, close to vertical—then the quantity of labor demanded and supplied will be only mildly responsive to the wage change.

The slopes of the curves are related to elasticities, and in this case they would show the relative change in the number of workers employed or seeking work given a relative change in the wage rate. In other words, what is the result of, say, a 1-percent change in the wage? If it produces more than a 1-percent change in the number of workers demanded, then we would say that the demand for labor is elastic—or highly responsive to wage costs. If it produces less than a 1-percent change in the number of workers demanded, then we would conclude that the demand for labor is inelastic—or less responsive to wages.

Elasticity estimates are vital to statistical analysis of the impact of minimum wages. The higher the elasticities, the greater the negative economic impact created by minimum wages. The lower the elasticities, the smaller will be the social costs imposed by minimum wages. Analysts who predict major negative impacts created by the minimum wage do so in part because they believe the elasticities are quite high; and the reverse tends to be true for analysts who conclude that minimum wages produce very small negative results.

But real life is complicated, and in addition the analyst should also consider functional shifts. These types of shifts have played a central role in recent studies investigating the impact on unemployment among teenage workers (Figure 13). If the wage rate is W_0, then the number of, say, teenage workers employed is N_1, given demand curve D_0 and supply curve S_0. But suppose the teenage population increases, so that the supply curve moves out from S_0 to S_1. This new supply function shows that—whatever the wage rate is—because of population increases, there will be a higher number of teenage workers seeking employment. If the minimum wage rate is raised by W_1, we might see unemployment among teenagers measured by N_4 minus N_0. But if there were no minimum wage, would there be any unemployment of teenagers?

The answer to that question hinges on one's perceptions about dynamic labor market operations and how equilibrium is achieved. If one believes that labor markets display a high degree of wage

61

Figure 13. Minimum wage impacts also depend on how demand and supply shift.

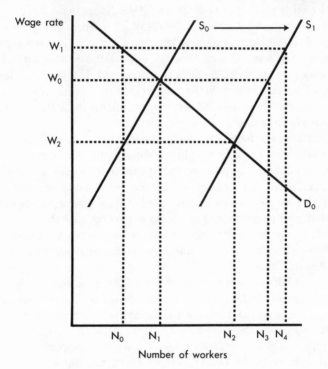

Number of workers

flexibility in response to excess demand or supply, then it would follow, everything else being the same, that in the absence of minimum wages there would not be any teenage unemployment. In a world of perfect wage flexibility the excess supply of labor (and resulting unemployment, measured by N_4 minus N_0) would drive down the wage rate to a new and lower equilibrium. Wages would fall to W_2, and with employment at N_2 there would be no unemployment.

However, this notion of perfect wage and price flexibility is far from an accurate reflection of the real world. Wages and prices often are sticky—what goes up does not easily or swiftly come down. Suppose that the price of labor is W_1. But because of wage rigidities, even if there were no minimum wages, the wage rate would not fall below W_0. Then as the supply curve shifted out to S_1, the resulting level of unemployment would be the distance between N_1 and N_3. In this world of wage rigidities, the minimum wage could not be blamed for the entire sum of unemployment. The minimum wage would have created only a smaller percentage of unemployment, which can be measured by subtracting the distance $N_1 N_3$ from $N_0 N_4$. In this case most of the unemployment would be the result of the shift in the supply function and *not* due to minimum wages.

The purpose of the geometric exposition is to demonstrate that the older conventional methodology used by researchers often created hazy pictures that hid as much information as they revealed. Using more refined analytical tools, economists have tried to separate the part of the absolute result due to minimum wages from the portion attributable to other factors, such as business conditions or population changes. In essence this mode of analysis tries to get at the structure of an economy.

Three Points of View

Given this standard economic theory, it should not be assumed that all—or even most—analysts have lined up on the same side concerning wage floor issues. In fact, throughout the interminable minimum wage debate, analysts have tended to be in one of three basic schools of thought concerning the impact of the statutory wage floor.

The first group views the minimum wage as extremely harmful for both the economy and the working poor. Leaning on neo-classical economic theory, this group has contended that the inevitable results of the minimum wage will be significant job losses and unemployment. According to the marginal productivity theory, profit-maximizing employers will hire workers as long as the value of their marginal productivity is greater than or equal to their costs. The minimum wage boosts a firm's wage bill but does not increase the productivity of its workers, and the net result is that a firm is forced to decrease its employment levels. Given the assumption that any job—no matter what the level of compensation—is better than being unemployed, the working poor are hurt by the minimum wages as more individuals are shoved into forced idleness. But there are also long-run injuries caused by the minimum wage. As labor becomes more expensive as a result of an increased wage floor, firms shift their investment towards more capital-intensive production processes that require fewer workers. This substitution of capital for labor can reduce long-term employment prospects. Since the working poor are the individuals who tend to have low productivity levels, it is these very workers who are fired from jobs—or not hired in the first place—as a consequence of the minimum wage.

At the other extreme is the view that the wage floor is an unmixed blessing for both the entire economy and the working poor. First, rejecting as myth the notion that all workers are paid according to their marginal productivity, the adherents to the all-blessing school have argued that in the real world wages of individual workers are determined mostly by historical patterns, customs, and institutions rather than by some arbitrary and usually undetermined measure of productivity. Second, because of their position in society, some workers are paid excessively low wages, and the result is larger-than-normal profits for their employers. A statutory minimum wage compels employers to increase the compensation paid to these workers and ends this form of exploitation. The net result will be reductions in excess profits, and the minimum wage will not create unemployment. Third, turning the productivity argument on its head, this group holds that a wage floor will result in improvements. As long as labor remains dirt cheap, a firm will have no real incentive to make the changes required to increase productivity. But faced with the wage floor, an employer will be forced to place a new value on labor, and this will result in productivity gains. Lastly, this school chides the neo-classicists for ignoring the overall ramifications of the floor on wages. Workers receiving low wages do not have the purchasing power to increase the demand for goods and services produced by the economy. This results not only in insufficient demand, slow growth levels, and recessions, but also in personal deprivation and accompanying social ills. A minimum wage can increase the purchasing power of workers and thus boost demand. Far from creating unemployment, a minimum wage can help in keeping the economy at full employment.

Between these two extremes is a third school that recognizes some truth on both sides. The minimum wage is neither an unmixed blessing nor an unmitigated evil. A wage floor involves tradeoffs. If it is set too high, then it may produce statistically significant unemployment; but if it is fixed at a moderate level, then the positive effects—gains in income and decreased exploitation of the working poor—may be greater than the negative impacts. Not to beg the question of defining moderation, advocates of the middle ground seem to rely upon experience and suggest that half of the average wage seems to have proved a reasonable base. This leaves unanswered the issue of universality. Some analysts within this group contend that while a moderate floor on wages might be the correct policy for most labor markets, exceptions might be in order—teenagers, for example—that require a different and lower minimum wage level. In the context of the modern welfare state there are income alternatives to wages. Instead of just viewing an individual as employed or unemployed, there is also the question of the level of compensation from work. Any job—no matter what the wages—might not be better than no job.

It would be comforting if the end product of the massive minimum wage studies would clearly indicate which one of these three positions is correct. If the results pointed toward the middle-of-the-road stance, we still would require actual quantitative estimates to describe what the magnitudes of the tradeoffs are in reality.

Deductive Reasoning

The limits reached by arguments based on economic theory, deductive logic, and only a casual examination of data were demonstrated in a famous exchange between two economists, George J. Stigler and Richard Lester, during the mid-1940s. Economic theory can be a powerful analytical tool, but without statistical testing it remains more a battle of faiths than a scientific debate.

Stigler argued that a minimum wage was bound to cause a good deal of harm and produce only very small benefits even for the working poor. Based on received economic theory, he reasoned that unless a minimum wage causes worker productivity to rise, a wage floor will force a profit-maximizing firm either to discharge workers or not to hire as many workers as it would in the absence of a minimum wage. Also, because of increased labor costs, firms will turn to more capital-intensive methods of production. Stigler felt there were several reasons for thinking that the minimum wage would not "shock" firms into increasing productivity levels. Generalizations based on a casual look at the data show that low-wage industries often are highly competitive. Also, these industries tend to have a high ratio of wages to total production costs. With strong competitive market pressures and a major percentage of costs represented by wages, these firms are already under the gun to make every productivity improvement possible. A minimum wage can not be expected to provide a significant added incentive. Without productivity increases, employment levels must decline.[3]

But even orthodox economists recognize that in some cases an employer may have a significant degree of control over the wage rate, and workers may be paid less than the value of their marginal productivity. In this situation a minimum wage, according to traditional economic theory, can both increase the wage paid to workers and raise employment levels. While admitting this possibility, economists clinging to the old religion would still contend that a uniform federal minimum wage cannot produce this result, given the diversity of conditions from firm to firm and industry to industry.

Typical of analysts who believe the statutory wage floor produces minimal negative impacts, Lester rejected economic theories based on marginal productivity. Recognizing that his methods and data were crude, he argued that conclusions based on assumptions of competitive wage determination fall short of describing and predicting real conditions. For example, investigations often show a wide range of wage rates being paid by firms in the same locality for the same kind of job. Lester insisted that there are very strong reasons for believing that a minimum wage will induce firms to increase productivity. Increased wage levels force management efficiency and encourage both training of workers and many alterations of existing production facilities in order to produce more with the firm's available resources. This means that the net result of a minimum wage is not increased unemployment.[4]

If the nation's gross national product is an increasing function of employment levels and a minimum wage reduces the number of workers employed, then a wage floor would reduce aggregate output. Neoclassical economists have used this deductive logic to make their case. But under Keynesian macroeconomic theories, a wage floor could increase worker purchasing power and result in higher levels of aggregate demand and gross national product.

A related issue raised by Stigler and others is that many people not considered to be part of the working poor are the beneficiaries of minimum wage increases. The relationship between family income and hourly wage rates is far from perfect. A minimum wage could increase the earnings of workers who are members of families with an income well above the national median. Pro-minimum wage analysts have concluded that the wage floor might not be the most perfectly efficient system one could dream of, but it is the best realistic tool for helping the working poor.

67

This debate, based mostly on intuition and deduction but very little data, settled few arguments. Following the trend toward quantitative research, minimum wage analysts have turned increasingly to subjecting their assumptions and conclusions to new data bases. Statistical testing is an attempt to increase our knowledge beyond the level of debate by logical deduction.

Minimum Wage Studies "B.C." (Before Computers)

Meager as the initial data were, the issues that emerged were reflected in the state and federal legislative debate and played a part in the formation of the minimum wage system. In real life the Solons could not afford the luxury of taking either extreme position—that minimum wages are all a blessing or an abomination. The legislation that emerged tended to be highly cautious, in line with the middle-of-the-road position. Low, or sweated, wages attested to the fact that some workers were being taken advantage of. A moderate minimum wage might help these workers and result in reductions of excess profits instead of reduced employment opportunities. But dramatic hikes in a company's wage bill might very well have an adverse effect on the workers the legislation was intended to help—by destroying their jobs. The early government-mandated studies were in a sense hedging on the bet. Once the laws were on the statute books, government researchers went out to take measurements before and after wage floor changes went into effect.

Pre-FLSA

The absolute before-and-after counting method was employed when state minimum wage laws were first introduced. For example, Oregon was one of the first states to enact a mandatory wage law covering women and minors. The U.S. Department of Labor Women's Bureau investigated the impact of the wage order by collecting data from forty retail stores in 1914—15. To meet the new wage orders, stores would have been required to increase their total payrolls by slightly over 1 percent. The researchers found that during the year after the wage order female employment in their sample of Oregon retail stores declined by almost 15 percent, while the number of male workers not subject to the wage order declined by almost 7.5 percent. A higher weekly minimum ordered for Portland required even larger changes. Female employment in the Portland area sampled declined by roughly 18 percent while male employment diminished by about 9 percent. In an area with a lower weekly minimum—for example, Salem—female employment in retail stores declined by 1 percent while male employment remained virtually unchanged.[5]

It is tempting to draw conclusions based on these studies. However the minimum wage is not the only factor that could explain the larger decline in female employment. When a recession hits, the last workers hired are often the first to be fired. In many cases seniority is the controlling factor considered in the decision of who will be laid off or recalled.[6] If the Oregon stores functioned under a seniority system and women in a majority of cases lacked seniority, then when sales declined a higher percentage of women than men would have been laid off even if there had been no minimum wage order. The data might not have reflected the impact of minimum wages, but rather they may have been the results of unrelated work practices.

Many other pre-FLSA studies followed this before-and-after absolute counting method. The picture we can draw from these types of investigations is hazy. There is not enough relevant data to test statistically different hypotheses bearing upon the impact of the wage floor.

Early FLSA

With the passage of the FLSA, added emphasis was placed on minimum wage investigation. Industry committees on a national level required data on proposed wage regulations. The congressional majority favored the elimination of excessively low wages, at least in covered industries, but at the same time it was concerned about the prospect of unemployment. In response to the legislative mandates, the Department of Labor reported to Congress on the results of the law. Government statistical investigations still concentrated on measuring absolute differences before and after a wage change.

Most of the minimum wage studies were at the industry level. An investigation of the seamless hosiery industry between 1938 and 1941 was representative of these studies. A 25-cent minimum wage became effective in 1938, and a wage order in 1939 raised the minimum to 32.5 cents an hour. This boost had a major impact, requiring a 10.1-percent direct increase in seamless hosiery payrolls. Based on a survey of ninety-one plants, the investigators found that the number of low-paid workers declined in absolute terms while the number of relatively high-paid employees increased. Workers paid below 25 cents in 1938 as a group experienced a decline of almost 15 percent in employment by the end of 1940. However, workers who were paid over 32.5 cents an hour in 1938 experienced employment gains as high as 12 percent by the close of the period. Yet a low-paid worker experienced a more than 40-percent increase in average hourly earnings.[7]

One researcher attempted to refine the before-and-after counting method by analyzing the changes in hours of work instead of just in total employment. From 1938 to 1939 workhours for the lowest paid employees declined by about 12 percent, while workhours for the highest paid group of workers increased by 23 percent.[8]

Other reports tried to examine the impact of minimum wages on regional wage differentials. With wages generally lower in the South than in the North, it would be expected that minimum wage impacts would not be uniform throughout the entire country. A Department of Labor study on workhours in men's cotton garment plants did record some differential impact. From 1939 to 1940 workhours in southern plants producing work clothing declined by about 16 percent, and in the North workhours diminished by roughly 3 percent. Meanwhile, in semidress pants manufacturing workhours increased by over 60 percent in the North but by only about 5 percent in the South.[9]

These changes in employment could be caused by other factors besides the wage floor. Yet this set of studies seemed to indicate that there were some employment effects associated with the minimum wage. The size of the changes was not clear, and the Department of Labor analysts concluded that they were not massive.

The 1950 Round

Government studies of the 1950 and 1956 minimum wage increases (from 40 cents to 75 cents an hour in 1950 and to $1 an hour in 1956) represented a second phase in wage floor investigations. After both increases the Department of Labor conducted expanded investigations of the economic impact due to the wage adjustments. Its conclusions were similar to the findings of earlier investigations. The report on the 1950 change concluded that the "industries studied . . . adjusted to the 75 cents rate with only minor effects other than the required pay increase."[10]

The 1950 study focused on five low-wage manufacturing industries: southern sawmilling, fertilizer, men's dress shirts and nightwear, men's seamless hosiery, and wood furniture. The investigation analyzed complaints that the increased minimum wage created plant shutdowns, and it also compared movements of hourly earnings in seventeen selected industries.

The Department of Labor researchers concluded that the boost in the minimum wage had no major employment effects on low-wage industries. Of the low-wage industries selected for study, only southern sawmilling, at 69 cents an hour, had an average hourly wage under the 75-cent minimum before the minimum wage increase. Having the lowest wage structure of the industries sampled, it was faced with the most challenging adjustments to the new minimum wage. From December 1949 to March 1950 average hourly earnings in the industry increased by 16 percent, and the wage differentials within the industry narrowed.

As far as employment is concerned, from the fourth quarter in 1949 to March 1950 the number of job holders in the southern sawmilling industry declined by 2 percent. Average hours declined from 42.8 to 40.7. The number of southern sawmills with eight employees or more remained virtually unchanged. Also, the researchers concluded that no sawmill operator who had closed down a plant held the 75-cent minimum wage solely responsible for the shutdown. As a result of the low-wage industry studies, the Department of Labor concluded that the higher minimum wage rate appeared to have a very minor effect on employment, plant shutdowns, prices, technological change, hiring practices, and overtime.

The Department of Labor study found that during the 13 years following the passage of the FLSA average hourly rates in covered low-wage industries rose more rapidly than wages in low-wage industries not covered by the FLSA or average wages in manufacturing. Since the official verdict by the Department of Labor analysts was that the minimum wage increase had a very small impact on all other economic variables, including employment, the conclusion was drawn that minimum wages had a very significant payoff by raising the relative wages of low paid workers, as follows:

	1938	1949	1950	1951	1938-51 increase (percent)
Selected high-wage industries	$0.89	$1.75	$1.80	$1.97	121
Selected low-wage industries covered by FLSA	$0.42	$1.01	$1.06	$1.14	171
Selected low-wage industries not covered by FLSA	$0.42	$0.88	$0.90	$0.95	126
All manufacturing industries	$0.62	$1.37	$1.42	$1.54	148

The conclusions were convincing only to true believers; skeptics raised questions about the validity of the methodology. Despite the fact that this study went into far greater detail than many previous investigations, it still lacked control groups. During 1950–51 other important variables did not remain the same. Within six months after the 75-cent hourly rate became law, the nation entered the Korean War, which was accompanied by an 8-percent rate of inflation within a year and the tightest labor market experienced in the United States since World War II.

The 1956 Round

The Department of Labor conducted an expanded study of the impact of FLSA when the minimum wage was increased to $1 in 1956. The major conclusions reached in this investigation were in line with the study of the 1950 increase—that the wage floor had not produced any significant economic harm. Several new techniques of analysis were introduced in this report.

The study assessed the macroeconomic impact of the wage floor. Before the increase the pay of about 2 million workers of the 24 million subject to the act was less than $1 an hour. The average increase required to bring a worker up to the new minimum was 15 cents an hour. The Labor Department analysts concluded that the minimum wage increase had not resulted in substantial changes in employment, or price levels. Workers who were being paid $1 or more before the increase did not get proportionate wage increases. The report also downplayed the impact of any ripple effect boosting the wage scale of the entire labor force.[11] Under the ripple effect, a worker whose wage is slightly above the minimum wage may receive an increase as the floor is raised. This would move the entire wage cluster up near the wage floor.

The Labor Department surveyed twelve manufacturing industries. The data pointed to some evidence of job loss as a result of minimum wages, but it gave no indication of its overall magnitude.

The industries most affected by the $1 minimum often appeared to have less favorable employment changes than other industries. Absolute employment did not decline for all of these industries, but employment in some of these sectors did not grow as fast as employment in other areas of the economy. To study the effect of the minimum wage, the researchers designed a *degree of impact index*, which expressed the percentage increase in a plant's average hourly earnings that would result if the earnings of all employees paid less than the $1 minimum wage were raised to $1. The index did not take into consideration the possibility that a higher minimum wage might cause a ripple effect on wages paid to workers who were receiving slightly above the minimum.

A simple example can show the meaning of this index. Suppose a plant employs four workers. Two of the workers are paid 75 cents an hour; one worker is paid $1.00 an hour; and the fourth worker is paid $1.50. Total hourly earnings at the plant would be $4.00, and the plant's average hourly earnings would be $1.00. If all wages were to be increased to $1 an hour, the two workers paid 75 cents an hour would each require a 25-cent raise. Total average hourly earnings in the plant would be $1.125, and the degree of impact index would be 12.5 (i.e., $1.125 divided by $1.00).

The researchers speculated that industries that had a high degree of impact index would also show the largest relative employment declines. The findings were mixed and often did not conform to this pattern. Some sectors with a low degree of impact showed greater declines in employment than sectors with a high degree of impact. Since the results were so mixed, the analysts concluded that the minimum wage could not explain the employment changes; if the minimum wage were such a strong force, the expected pattern would have been seen. However, this study seemed to change nobody's opinion. Pro-minimum wage forces claimed that the degree of impact study indicated that they were correct, while opponents interpreted the data as bolstering their case. This analysis included more statistical detail than many previous studies, but it still did not control for other variables, or economic forces, and it did not end the minimum wage debate.

In the same study the Department of Labor also investigated the employment results in low-wage labor markets by collecting employment data in small cities one month before and three months after the minimum wage raise. Employment increased in three out of the seven cities and declined in four, as follows:[12]

City	Change in number of workers in covered industries (percent)
Fort Smith, Arkansas	+4.8
Athens, Georgia	+2.1
Dothan, Alabama	+0.6
Meridian, Mississippi	−1.5
Dalton, Georgia	−4.4
Sunbury-Shamokin-Mt. Carmel, Pennsylvania	−4.9
Hickory, North Carolina	−5.5

On the basis of this information it might be argued that minimum wages have at most only a small negative impact on employment even in labor markets with large concentrations of low-wage workers. However, some economists question whether this is a correct judgment when other data are considered. The mix of industries was quite different in the cities surveyed. If business conditions were not at the same level in all industries, then it would be hard to make any uniform comparisons among cities.

For example, lumber, wood products, and food industries accounted for employment concentrations in Dothan, Alabama, and Meridian, Mississippi. Each of these industries experienced national employment growth rates of about 1 percent, but both cities had employment rates under this national level. A case could be made that, instead of having a minor or no impact, the minimum held down employment opportunities in these communities to rates under the national level. Hickory, North Carolina, had a major concentration in textile and apparel workers. In the period investigated national employment declined in these sectors 2 and 5 percent, respectively; yet Hickory's employment loss rate was larger than the national for these industries. Hence it could be argued that the data do show a strong negative minimum wage impact.[13] The time period examined might not have been long enough for the effects to take place. The point is that data on city employment changes are not adequate if they do not also consider percentage differences in employment by industries and shifting patterns in national demand and supply for various products.

The 1960s—Extended Coverage

During the 1960s the number of workers covered by the FLSA was vastly increased. Investigators paid greater attention to the impact of minimum wages on newly covered industries. In general, the Department of Labor investigations found that the expanded FLSA protection had no major negative economic impact on the newly covered workers. As before, the Department of Labor counted the absolute changes in employment before and after a new segment of the labor force was included in the minimum wage program.

The 1961 FLSA amendments extended coverage to some 3.5 million additional workers, many of whom were employed in the retail sector. Also, the law changed the traditional test of coverage from an employee's particular activity to the coverage of all employees of an enterprise in which some workers were covered. The amendments also introduced a volume-of-sales test as a measure of an enterprise's interstate activity. However, to ease the adjustment process for newly covered sectors, the amendments set up a different schedule of minimum wages in these industries. The minimum wage for workers covered prior to 1961 was set at $1.15, to be raised to $1.25 two years later. Meanwhile, the newly covered workers were scheduled to receive a minimum wage of

$1.00 an hour in 1961, which was to be raised in steps to $1.25 by 1965.

The Labor Department concluded that the impact of these amendments was to produce significant wage increases in most newly covered areas without causing significant unemployment. It should not come as a surprise that these exact two points were the congressionally stated objectives of the FLSA amendments. Hence, the Labor Department was telling Congress that it had hit the nail on the head—that Congress had accomplished exactly what it initially intended to do. A survey of fifteen nonmetropolitan areas in the South, where the 1961 amendments might be expected to have had a major negative impact, found that employment in these areas increased by 9 percent from 1960 to 1964. The increase in employment for these southern areas was twice as great as the gains in employment nationwide for nonagricultural industries during this period. Extension of coverage was judged as not curtailing employment for these areas.[14]

In 1963 the FLSA was amended to prohibit discrimination in pay because of sex. The 1966 amendments further extended coverage to some 9 million workers, mostly in the retail and service industries. Studies of newly covered industries led the Labor Department to conclude once again that the FLSA amendments did not cause economic disruptions. Government researchers found little or no evidence of layoffs or plant shutdowns related to the minimum wage increases.[15]

Hotel and restaurant studies showed that employment increased after the minimum wage in the covered part of the industry but declined in the uncovered portion. That the decline in the uncovered portion might be due to a long-term trend centering on a reduction in the number of smaller hotel facilities was not statistically tested. Coverage was also extended to certain sectors of the agricultural industry, but these newly covered workers were also placed on a lower minimum wage schedule than previously covered workers. Labor Department studies found that farm employment continued a secular decline after these amendments. But the decrease in employment on covered farms was only one-third as great as on noncovered farms. However, other factors besides minimum wages might explain these results.

The Labor Department under the Nixon and Ford administrations also reached similar conclusions. In 1970 then Secretary of Labor George P. Shultz reported that "educational and hospital sectors had little evident difficulty adjusting to the minimum wages established by the 1966 amendments."[16] But the flaw of the methodology used in these reports is clearly shown in the hospital, medical, and educational areas. The 1966 amendments were passed one year after the enactment of Medicare and Medicaid and the passage of the Elementary and Secondary Education Act. These measures expanded employment in these industries, and it should not come as a surprise that these areas easily adjusted to the 1966 FLSA amendments, particularly since Uncle Sam had started to pick up an increasing portion of the tab. Using similar testing methods, the Department of Labor also concluded that minimum wage increases had not significantly contributed to any inflationary spiral. The judgment was based on a comparison of price differentials in selected northern and southern areas.[17]

In 1971 then Secretary of Labor James D. Hodgson reported that employment in newly covered sectors often fared better than in industries that were not greatly affected by FLSA amendments.[18] A year later he reported that mandated minimum wage increases "had no discernible adverse effect on overall employment levels."[19] For example, a departmental study of hired farm workers found that between 1968 and 1971 employment declined by 21 percent in the uncovered subsector of the industry and by 9 percent in the covered portion.[20] Yet these data might have nothing to do with minimum wages; they might instead only reflect long-run trends toward the consolidation of farms. Since the FLSA amendments applied only to larger farms, it is reasonable to expect that—regardless of the minimum wage—the larger farms continued to grow while smaller units showed sharper employment declines.

Findings based on this methodology, despite its flaws, have played a major role in the growing debate over minimum wages. The AFL-CIO and other minimum wage advocates have been quick to note that repeated government studies—under both Democratic and Republican administrations—have found only a very few isolated instances of adverse economic effects caused by minimum wages.[21]

What have we learned from these studies? Many observers have answered this question by saying, Not much! But this fails to take into consideration who was ordering the studies and why they were conducted in the first place. The findings assured policy-makers that the floor on wages for covered industries was not wreaking havoc on the economy and that the unemployment impact of the minimum wage was not massive. The size of any negative results appeared to be small enough to be politically manageable. Also, the studies seemed to indicate that the system could easily withstand moderate increases in the wage floor. In this sense, the studies brought solace to policymakers and in many ways told them what they wanted to hear.

4

The Computer to the Rescue?

Modeling for the Calculator

The shortcomings of the early FLSA assessments reflect the tools that were available at the time. But as data sources expanded and computers rendered calculations in seconds instead of weeks, minimum wages were subjected to more comprehensive tests. The motivation behind these newer studies appears to be threefold: First, traditional economists sought empirical data to support their economic theories concerning minimum wages; second, researchers hoped that, with the new technology in hand, they would be able to produce accurate quantitative estimates on the wage floor impacts; and third, there was the idea that the new technology had a life, or driving force, of its own—God would not have given humanity the computer if it was not to be used on minimum wages.

In this new state of minimum wage analysis, researchers attempt to design statistical models as the best available substitute for laboratory controls. However, before we examine the products of the new technology, a brief review of the estimation techniques most often used in these investigations is in order.

Estimation Techniques

Even given basic economic theory, including such notions as a demand and supply function, there still remains the crucial process of determining the shapes of these lines. An analyst's results are highly dependent upon where the lines are drawn and the shape of the functions. Statistics and econometrics are the tools that are used to try to answer these series of questions. Based on empirical data, these estimation techniques attempt to picture the position and characteristics of key economic relationships.

Economists most often use regression analysis to estimate the impact of minimum wages. Using this methodology the analyst tries to estimate or fit the best line, or mathematical equation, to the available data. The data collected will show, say, the relationship between wage rates and the number of workers hired. The problem facing the analyst is to determine the mathematical equation that best fits the scatter of points. Since statistical analysis is based on probability, the equation, or demand curve, will not contain every observation. Some of the points will be off the line. But the goal is to estimate a line, or curve, to which most of the observations are quite close. The analyst might try the following simple equation:

Employment = A + B (wage rate) + Error

In this equation, A is a parameter that might represent other economic factors. B is the coefficient of the wage rate; it shows the responsiveness of employment to changes in the wage rate, indicating the elasticity, or the relative responsiveness of employment to wages. The last term, the error, takes into account that the equation is only an approximation of reality. Employment, since it depends upon the wage rate in this equation, is called the dependent variable. The wage rate is the independent variable.

Given some employment and wage rate data, the analyst's task is to estimate A, B, and the error. The method most often used to produce the best-fitting equation is to find the equation that produces the smallest error. Suppose the data are fed into a computer and the computer is told to find the best-fitting equation. The result might be as follows:

Employment $= 10,000 - 3$ (wage rate)

If the wage rate is $1, then the equation would estimate that employment would be 9,997 workers. If the wage rate were $10, the employment estimate would be 9,970. The analyst could now draw an estimated demand curve. Since the equation is only an approximation, the investigator might be interested in the percentage of the data that is "explained" by the estimate. The computer might find that the estimated equation explains, say, 85 percent of the data. This would mean that there still remains 15 percent not taken into account. The confidence the analyst may place in the results could depend upon how much of the data can be explained by the equation.

Besides considering the statistical significance of the entire equation the analyst should not ignore the statistical significance of each individual estimated variable. For example, the estimate for the wage coefficient was -3. Since the estimation technique is based on probability—not certainty—and since the entire equation is only an approximation, the real number might fluctuate below or above 3. Statistical estimation techniques provide measurements for the degree of confidence that can be placed in an estimated number. The computer might calculate that there is a very high probability, say 95 percent, that the real number lies between -2.75 and -3.25, or it might be that the estimate of -3 has no statistical significance. The real value of the variable could be zero, which would mean that the wage rates may have no impact on employment levels.

Once an analyst derives a regression equation based on past data and events, the temptation is to make predictions on the assumption that the past is prologue to the future. Given this equation, what will be the employment level if the wage increases to some higher rate? The regression equation was based on combinations of observations on both wages and employment levels. Now the analyst would be using only wage figures to predict future employment totals. There are clear dangers in these predictions. First, the regression equation shows estimated relationships that have existed in the past. There is no law mandating that these relationships, even if correctly estimated for past events, will hold true in the future. Second, predictions often require extrapolation of equations beyond the range of reliable data. What was true when the wage rate was between $2.00 and $3.00 might not hold if the wage rate reaches $4.50. Extrapolating beyond the range of data is fraught with uncertainties.

Most statistical minimum wage studies that employ these techniques are more complicated than outlined here. The demand equation considered only wages, but there may be many other variables that influence employment levels. Multiple regression techniques might be used to estimate the following type of demand curve:

$$\text{Employment} = A + B\,(\text{wage rate}) + C\,(\text{profit rate}) + D\,(\text{business conditions}) + E\,(\text{imports}) + \text{Error}$$

Employment levels would now depend, not only upon the wage rate, but also upon profit rates, business conditions, and imports. Although this equation is more complex than the first equation, it could be estimated by using similar methods. The coefficients B, C, and D would show the importance of the different independent variables in determining employment levels.

The multiple regression is a proxy for a controlled experiment. When employment changes, the analyst could try to use this regression to estimate what portion of the employment differences was due to wage changes, profit shifts, changes in business conditions, or fluctuations in imports. A multiple regression shares with the simple equation the same problems when predicting future events. Relationships that held in the past might not be exactly the same in the future. Also, predictions for the future often require extrapolation beyond the observed data.

What Is an Economic Model?

To understand why various researchers may reach different conclusions from presumably the same data, it is necessary to examine the components of an economic model. A main cause of the wide-ranging estimates is that there are different assumptions contained in models. For many people the word *model* creates pictures of toy trains, airplanes, building blocks, or centerfolds; but in the natural and social sciences a model is not just a miniature representation of something in the larger world. In the sciences a model is a hypothetical, or imagined, construct used to explain data and make predictions. An economic model in essence has four main parts: definitions, structural form, reduced form, and data.

Definitions, or identities, must be established. For example, the multiple regression equation contained a variable for business conditions. Is the gross national product a good measure of the level of business activity? If GNP is to be the measure, will it be based on current dollar values, or will it be a figure that has been adjusted to take into account inflation? What is meant by unemployment? This is no idle quibble, since the Department of Labor publishes seven different unemployment indexes.

The second part of an economic model consists of structural equations. A simple model might look at the structure of demand and supply equations as follows:

Demand for labor = A + B (wage rate) + C (profit rate) + D (business conditions)
Supply of labor = E + F (wage rate) + G (population age 16 years and over) + H (unearned income)

Researchers often employ vastly different structures. Despite its speed and agility, the electronic genie only does what it is told to do. For example, an estimated supply equation could be very different depending upon whether it contains a variable for population. An equation that does not contain a population variable might show that the wage rate has a major impact on the supply of labor, when some of this impact may in fact be due to population shifts that would be detected if this variable were included in the model. Structural equations contain basic assumptions about the operations of the economy, including the variables that should be considered.

The way the demand for labor function is stated contains several basic assumptions, one of which is that profit rates and business conditions are two distinct independent forces that establish employment levels. It might be argued that these variables are not independent and that they in fact interact in establishing a level of employment. One way of representing this interaction statistically is to multiply the two variables to form a third. This would create the following structural equation, which would be quite different from the first:

Demand for labor = A + B (wage rate) + C (profit rate) X (business conditions)

The results might vary depending upon the structure used. A second group of differences are the lags built into a model. It takes time, just like an aspirin tablet, before a variable has an impact on the system. The analyst might assume that demand for labor during a given calendar quarter depends upon the business conditions and profit rates experienced in the previous quarter. But might not the lag be an average of conditions that existed during the previous two quarters? It takes time for an increased minimum wage to work its impact on an economy. How one treats this lag can influence the findings.

Many analysts do not directly estimate their structural equations, but instead they estimate a reduced form equation. The need for a reduced form equation can be demonstrated from the above simple structural equations. The wage rate is included in both the demand and the supply equations, and this variable has a direct impact on both functions. As Alfred Marshall insisted, the demand and supply equations are like two blades of a scissors: both blades cut the paper at the same time. In a similar fashion a reduced form equation attempts to estimate the interactions of the demand and supply functions at the same time. It tries to give a clear and direct path of causation. To estimate the structural equations directly would be like saying that only one blade of the scissors cuts the paper while ignoring the impact of the second blade. With estimates for a reduced form equation, an analyst attempts to work the problem backwards, in a sense, and then estimates the structural part of the model.

The analyst must look at the interaction of supply and demand (i.e., the adjustment process). One simple form might be to assume an equilibrium condition in which the demand for labor always equals the supply. Different models contain various forms of this supply and demand interaction. In a world that does not demonstrate rapid wage and price flexibility, the interaction of demand and supply will be highly complex.

Given the definitions, structural equations, and reduced form, an analyst still is left with a crucial decision about the selection of the data that should be used to form model estimates. The analyst may decide to use—depending upon the occasion and the availability of data—cross-sectional, time series, longitudinal, or experimental data. The results might very well hinge on the type of data that is employed. *Cross-sectional data* are like a snapshot providing a picture of conditions at a specific period of time. *Time series data* are like a movie picture portraying motion over time; however, in this type of data series, the actual people who are in the sample are not constant. *Longitudinal data* attempt to follow a specific cohort over some time period. Last, *experimental data* are real observations recorded from an actual experiment. Minimum wage estimates can depend on the type of data used. For example, labor supply estimates have varied depending on the type of data used.

Often the specific data that a model requires do not exist. In this case econometricians may be forced to use a proxy for the variable they would really like to measure. Recent models have often assumed that labor demanded by companies depends upon expected future sale, prices, and inflation rates. In this case researchers have to construct a proxy of what employers' expectations are. One assumption might be that whatever the current rate of inflation, business executives expect this rate to continue during the next quarter of the year. The results depend upon the proxy used.

Once the regression equations of the economic model are estimated, analysts try to predict the future impact of some proposed change, such as an increase in the minimum wage. This use of an economic model is called a simulation. For example, given past data and estimates of what the other independent variables will be, the analysts may try to predict the results of a 20-percent boost in the minimum wage. A simulation based on an econometric model tries to capture all the direct and indirect effects caused by a government policy. The answers and estimates produced by a simulation are based on all the steps outlined above in the construction of an economic model.

Teenagers

The new technology has been used to examine teenage labor markets more than any other segment of the work force. Even if the minimum wage were to have a small negative impact on the entire labor force, it still might have a major effect on individuals with the least skills or lowest productivity, assumed to be young workers. The ratio of teenage to adult unemployment has risen during the post–World War II period, and the minimum wage is often blamed for higher youth unemployment. If this is the case, then rising

87

minimum wage rates should be able to explain a good part of teenage unemployment. There is also a political reality behind narrowing the focus on teenage labor markets. Under current political conditions, Congress is not about to junk the FLSA. But while successive administrations and congresses have appeared willing to retain minimum wage protection for most adult workers, some analysts have championed a subminimum wage for teenage workers. Econometric investigations showing a good deal of harm caused to younger workers by the minimum wage would bolster the case for a subminimum. Since politics is the art of the possible, it is only natural to concentrate one's efforts on a subgroup of the labor force where change is considered probable.

However, as with most controversial issues, economists can not agree about the true magnitude of the changes brought about by minimum wages. An examination of a few specific investigations demonstrates the divergent estimates reached by different analysts.

Thomas Gale Moore has argued that the minimum wage has caused teenage unemployment.[1] He reasoned that if overall labor market conditions get worse, then teenage unemployment should move in the same direction. The higher the minimum wage rate is as a percentage of the general wage level, the more teenage unemployment should be recorded. Also, teenage unemployment should increase as wage floor coverage is expanded to more industries. These are the expected qualitative results, but what is important is the size of each force and the length of time it will take employers to make adjustments. Employers may prefer attritions to layoffs, and it takes time to substitute capital and skilled workers for unskilled workers. Also, a higher minimum wage might attract more teenagers into the labor market in an effort to find work. The net result, according to this model, should be higher teenage unemployment rates. Inflation, on the other hand, may be a countervailing force reducing the statutory minimum wage as a percent of average wages.

Using monthly teenage white and nonwhite male and female unemployment rates from January 1954 to July 1968, Moore concluded that the minimum wage was a statistically significant factor contributing to the rise of youth unemployment. The model also simulated the magnitude of the impact. Moore estimated that if the unemployment rate of nonwhite teenagers was 20 percent and the minimum wage was set at 50 percent of the average hourly wage, a boost of 10 percent in the wage floor would increase nonwhite teenage unemployment to 22 percent. A higher minimum wage would result in a statistically significant jump in teenage unemployment rates. The impact on white teenagers would be about two-thirds less than on nonwhite teenagers, although it would still be significant. But this increased unemployment would not show up overnight. About 43 percent of the teenage unemployment created by an increased minimum wage would become manifest in one year, and 83 percent of the minimum wage impact would have worked itself through the system by the end of three years. These estimates were based on the statistical lags used in the model.

However, Moore suggested that his model, using official statistics, might understate the real impact of minimum wages on teenage unemployment. When unemployment increases, many nonwhite teenagers become discouraged about finding work and leave the labor market. Such teenage workers were not recorded in the official unemployment rate, and this yielded lower estimates. Moore found, however, that the adverse impacts of minimum wages apply to teenagers only. As the youths mature, they gain work experience and skills and are no longer as directly affected by minimum wage legislation.

Other economic models have also detected negative minimum wage impacts on teenage labor markets. For example, Douglas K. Adie employed a more complex nonlinear mathematical model assuming that the impact of minimum wage legislation may be exponential instead of uniform.[2] He assumed that the demand for

89

teenage workers was a function of the Federal Reserve Board's industrial production index multiplied by the real minimum wage adjusted for inflation. Accordingly, he first estimated unemployment elasticities for different groups of teenagers. The goal was to find the relative change in unemployment levels, given a stated increase in the minimum wage. Assuming an unemployment rate of 20 percent, Adie estimated that a 10-percent increase in the minimum wage would result in significantly higher unemployment rates for nonwhites, as follows:

Group	Resulting unemployment rate (percent)
All teenagers	22.7
White teenagers	22.3
Nonwhite teenagers	26.0
Female white teenagers	22.5
Male nonwhite teenagers	25.0
Female nonwhite teenagers	27.6

The model estimated that 40 months would elapse before the unemployment impact of minimum wages was completely absorbed, but the brunt of the negative impact would be felt between eight and sixteen months after the increase in the minimum wage.

For those who believe that minimum wages create teenage unemployment, there is something heartening about the Moore and Adie models. Both conclude that the minimum wage does in fact produce a statistically significant level of youth unemployment. However, they differ sharply about the magnitude of the impact. The estimated direction of the investigations might be the same, but their quantitative findings are quite different. Given a 20-percent unemployment rate among nonwhite teenagers, a 10-percent increase in the minimum wage produces an unemployment rate of 22 percent in the first model. The same change results in a 26-percent unemployment rate for nonwhite teenagers in the second model. This is a large difference, and the error between the two estimates is more than 18 percent. Economic policy formulation might strive for more accurate estimates of a variable's size as well as its direction.

A close scrutiny would show that the conclusions of both models were based on a narrow range of variables. These types of models are guilty of the same basic fault that was placed at the door of earlier investigations. Granted that the former never laid claim to have conducted controlled experiments, the newer studies in reality have not necessarily controlled for many more variables than the discounted older reports did.

Certainly, any analysis of minimum wage impacts on teenagers during the 1960s and 1970s should not ignore the obvious supply factors. During the 1960s the United States population 16 to 19 years of age increased by some 40 percent to 15.3 million, which compares with a 12-percent growth in the entire population during this period. Supply factors should also be considered in analysis of minimum wages for the 1980s. The boom period in teenage population growth is over, and the 1980s will witness a decline of about 8.5 percent in the teenage population. If these and other factors were considered, it might be shown that the minimum wage does not have a major statistically significant impact on teenage unemployment rates. The effects of the minimum wage cannot be understood in isolation from other economic, political, and demographic events.

A prime example of a more ambitious model was detailed in a 1969 study conducted by the United States Department of Labor. The Nixon administration favored a subminimum wage for teenage workers. But not relying on gut reactions, Secretary of Labor George Shultz directed the Bureau of Labor Statistics (BLS) to undertake a comprehensive study of the relationship between the minimum wage program and youth unemployment rates. The BLS employed the regression methodology outlined above. But unlike the two other models which claimed to have demonstrated the injurious effects of minimum wage on the basis of a few selected variables, the BLS model took into account population shifts, migration patterns, and government programs that might have an impact on teenage labor markets.

The "enriched" BLS model, designed by Hyman B. Kaitz, also departed from previous studies in defining unemployment. Instead of confining the study to the civilian labor force, the model considered the percentage of unemployed teenagers within the entire population. There is a significant difference in these two concepts. With shifting labor force participation rates, correlation between the size of the population and the labor force is far from perfect. With the changes in nonmarket activities, such as school and military service, the size of the civilian labor force and of the population could even move in different directions. Since education and military service are, for many teenagers, alternatives to working in the civilian labor force, it would seem reasonable to take into account these socially useful options in calculating the ratio of forced idleness. Also, the relative size of the teenage population compared with the entire population has not remained constant during the post–World War II era. This factor could also cause problems if a growing relative number of teenagers enter the labor force seeking jobs.[3]

The BLS model measured both unemployment and employment ratios for various groups of teenagers, including 16- to 17-year-olds and 18- to 19-year-olds, males and females, and whites and nonwhites. The model assumed that these ratios depended upon several policy variables controllable by the government and on other independent economic forces that the government can influence only indirectly. Ratios of minimum wage rates to average hourly earnings by industry were combined into an index that gave added weight to a sector of the economy that was highly covered by the FLSA and employed a large percentage of teenagers.

On the assumption that the military draft, rising school attendance, and expanding federal government manpower programs might have a significant impact on teenage labor markets, the influence of these programs was also included in the equations. The unemployment rate of adult males was used as a proxy of the general level of economic activity.

The study also investigated other factors besides the minimum wage that contribute to unemployment. Accordingly, the study explored whether the postwar baby boom, which vastly increased the number of teenagers, might be the culprit in teenage unemployment by causing the supply of teenagers to outpace the demand. In an effort to test this theory, the model contained variables representing teenage population changes. Beyond examining aggregate population changes, the study considered shifts in the relative portion of nonwhite youths. Another variable considered was population shifts out of rural into urban areas, which might also be expected to create unemployment problems for teenagers. To investigate this labor force aspect, the model contained measures of agricultural employment among teenagers as a proxy for this population shift.

On the basis of this structure and assumptions, the BLS study concluded that the general level of economic activity had the strongest impact on teenage unemployment and employment ratios. Shifts in business conditions, as measured by the adult unemployment rate, were the most important variable in explaining changes in teenage labor markets. In many cases the supply of teenagers also had a significant impact on employment and unemployment ratios.

Given all these considerations, the estimated impact of minimum wages on teenage unemployment and employment ratios was clouded, to say the least. Traditional economic theory has held that as the minimum wage goes up, teenage unemployment will increase and youth employment will be reduced if all other variables are held constant. However, many of the estimated equations indicated that the opposite might have happened. Even when other factors were controlled, the model predicted that a 25-percent hike in the minimum wage would *decrease* the unemployment rate by 0.1 percentage points—or essentially no change.

The BLS model builders suggested several reasons why the minimum wage impact appeared often to move in the opposite direction from what was expected. The minimum wage may have reduced the employment opportunities for 16- to 17-year-olds, and this would improve the relative standing of 18- to 19-year-olds. Many teenagers may want a job but decide not to look for one because they believe that an employment search would be fruitless. The minimum wage may increase the number of discouraged young workers, and these conditions were not measured under the model's definition of unemployment. Since most of the minimum wage estimates did not show a high degree of statistical significance, little trust can be placed in these specific numbers. However, if the minimum wage was a prime cause of teenage unemployment, one would expect that the estimates would demonstrate a very large degree of statistical significance. Since this was not the case, one might question how important the minimum wage is in either predicting or explaining teenage unemployment or employment ratios.

Teenage population shifts, school enrollment rates, and rural-to-urban movements tended to have some estimated measurable impact on teenage labor markets. In several cases, government manpower programs were also judged to be important.

Other studies that took into account the variables considered by the Bureau of Labor Statistics, or related factors, estimated that minimum wages have a very small statistical significance on teenage labor markets. A model constructed by Hugh Folk tried to explain and predict teenage unemployment rates and labor force participation levels. Minimum wages were one set of variables in the equations. In over 60 percent of the estimates produced by this model the minimum wage variable did not even show the direction expected by traditional economic theory. The impact of minimum wages was estimated to be insignificant.[4]

Several economists have attempted to reanalyze the data used in the minimum wage models.[5] It appears that the essential difference lies in the type of explanatory variables that are included in a model.[6] The impact of demographic variables appears to be a powerful factor causing the different conclusions. Inclusion of demographic factors dilutes the influence that can be attributed to minimum wages on teenage unemployment.

A model that ignores the growth in supply during the 1960s and 1970s will tend to show that minimum wages play a significant role in creating teenage unemployment. However, a model that includes these demographic variables in the basic equations will tend to show that minimum wages have had a minor, or at best secondary, impact on teenage unemployment rates. In such a model the most important variable in explaining teenage unemployment and employment rates will tend to be some proxy of general business conditions.

Analysts who ignored demographic variables in analyzing the impact of minimum wages have argued that ascribing teenage unemployment to an excess supply of young workers ignores laws of supply and demand. If demand varies little—or does not grow as fast as supply—then the wages paid to teenagers should fall, with the result that a new market equilibrium at a lower wage rate is achieved. If the statutory floor does not permit the price of labor to decline, then minimum wages prevent the laws of supply and demand from functioning. Using this logic, teenage unemployment could be placed at minimum wage's doorstep even when demographic factors are considered—because the price of young labor is too high.

However, logic that applies to markets for eggs and butter often does not apply to labor markets, where the commodity is human beings. The application of supply and demand arguments assumes that we live in a world of wage flexibility. But American labor markets do not normally demonstrate wage flexibility in the downward direction. Pointing to the minimum wage as the culprit accounting for a major portion of teenage unemployment reflects more ideology than an objective examination of the facts. The evidence

95

indicates that economic models that disregarded changes in demographic forces may have failed to consider a prime factor influencing labor markets during the 1960s and 1970s.

Beyond Unemployment Effects

The models investigated so far considered only the employment aspects of minimum wages. These are important, certainly, but the minimum wage might be expected to produce other results as well. When the minimum wage is increased, an employer might not lay off workers and may instead resort to some other responses to counteract added costs of labor. Models that deal with large statistical aggregates often may not detect shifts other than changes in employment and unemployment. One methodology that can uncover other effects is to study the minimum wage question at the establishment level, in keeping with the microeconomic theory that a firm has several options in reaction to a boost in the cost of a factor of production, such as labor.

The potential benefits of case studies are illustrated by an investigation examining the impact of a 1957 increase in the New York state minimum wage covering retail stores. At the time the federal wage floor did not provide protection to this sector of the economy. The New York state order set the retail store minimum wage at $1.00 per hour in larger cities and 90 cents in the rest of the state. About 25 percent of the retail stores in the state were estimated to be affected by this wage order, and in the affected stores roughly 36 percent of the workers required wage increases. Less than 1 percent of the state retail work force was laid off or quit.[7] However, statewide aggregates offered only a partial, not to say blurred, picture. For example, while for the entire industry the increase in direct payroll costs was 3.1 percent, small retail stores often had to meet a much higher percentage boost in direct costs.

A Cornell University research team complemented the statewide study by analyzing the responses of individual retail stores to the wage hike. The goal was to obtain more detailed information than was included in the large-scale investigation. The study picked forty-two retail stores in the Syracuse and Auburn areas. One-quarter of these stores had to increase their payrolls by an average of 16 percent to meet the wage order. For all stores sampled the average increase in payrolls required to meet the state order was 7.7 percent. However, these percentage figures assumed that the stores kept their employees and did not change work hours or other work-related practices. In fact, the study found that the sampled stores frequently made varied adjustments to compensate for paying higher wages to workers who had been earning less than the new minimum. In half of the stores, no wages were raised any higher than the new minimum level by the time the order had been in effect for four months. The sampled retail stores absorbed about 60 percent of the increased costs in payrolls due to the minimum wage. Employers found many different ways to offset the remaining 40 percent of the cost increase. The most frequent method used in offsetting the remaining 40 percent was the adjustment of employee hours. The second most widely used tool to offset costs was to lay off workers, and the workers who were fired tended to be the elderly, part-timers, and the handicapped. Only 1 percent of workers sampled were fired. Yet 4.5 percent of those workers who had previously earned under $1 an hour lost their jobs.[8]

Besides adjusting hours and discharging some workers, the 40-percent offset in costs was also accomplished by curtailing store hours, changing job assignments, and attempting in other ways to increase workers' productivity. Several stores increased employee training and improved their selection process for hiring workers. By using these adjustments, many stores were able to increase their labor productivity, or output per work hour, and in part offset the cost of the wage order. None of the stores went out of business, but smaller stores tended to have a harder time offsetting the cost increase than larger units did. Only five of the forty-two stores sampled claimed that prices were increased because of the wage order. However, it should be noted that overall retail sales in the two cities surveyed showed a decline during this period, and in a time of improved business conditions firms might have been able to pass off more of the cost increase on to consumers. Also, retail trade tends to be a fairly competitive sector of the economy. One might expect that in a more highly concentrated industry, with fewer but larger firms, companies would be able to shift a greater percentage of the increased cost in the form of higher prices to the consumer.

There are several lessons to be learned from this approach. An increase in the minimum wage sets various forces in motion, and individual firms have many options. There may be some loss of job opportunities, but firms may absorb some of the increased cost. Also, a wage floor seems to provide an inducement to employers to increase their labor productivity. However, productivity gains did not erase the total cost of the wage hike. Beyond changing the number of workers, firms may also adjust work hours, the mix of full-time and part-time labor force, and employee training. By exclusively counting employment or unemployment, a researcher fails to detect other important changes induced by the minimum wage.

In fact, recent econometric models support this conclusion. Studies by Edward Gramlich indicate that the minimum wage forces some young workers out of full-time jobs and into part-time employment.[9] Jobs in the latter group tend to provide fewer chances for advancement, lower wage, and less training than full-time positions.[10] Even if a teenager did not become unemployed as a result of the minimum wage, the wage floor could influence the current kind of job and the economic future of the youth.

Another impact of the minimum wage may be to make teenagers and low-wage workers increasingly vulnerable to the hardship caused by an economic recession. Marvin Kosters and Finis Welch analyzed this possibility by suggesting that adverse employment effects caused by minimum wages may be inadvertently considered a result of cyclical declines.[11] When an economy is booming, they reasoned, productivity tends to rise as production facilities and workers operate at maximum efficiency. However, during a recession productivity may decline as plants and the labor force are inefficiently used or kept in a state of partial idleness.[12]

Assume that a teenage worker's productivity is equal to $3.00 an hour when the economy is in a boom period, while an adult worker's productivity level is $4.00 an hour and the minimum wage $2.90. When a recession strikes, marginal productivity of both declines to, say, $2.75 for the teenager and $3.75 for the adult. In good times the firm found it profitable to employ the young worker, but in a recession the mandated minimum wage would dictate laying off the young worker or suffering a loss. Meanwhile, since the adult worker's productivity is far above the minimum wage level even in a recession, the older worker retains his or her job.

To test their hypothesis Kosters and Welch examined employment data between 1954 and 1968. They found a high relative vulnerability of youth labor markets to general business conditions. A 1-percent decline in aggregate employment resulted in a 3.5-percent decline in teenage employment but a reduction of only 0.8 percent in adult employment.

In support of their thesis that youth are hurt by the minimum wage, Kosters and Welch argued that the employment levels of workers classified by age, color, and sex depended upon *normal employment*, defined as the long-term growth in the number of jobs for a specific class of workers, and *transitional employment*, defined as the difference between actual employment at a given time and normal employment. During the 14-year period they examined, teenagers accounted for 6.3 percent of total normal employment and 22.1 percent of all transitional employment. They calculated that in a contraction a teenager is four times as likely to lose his or her job as an adult worker. Nonwhite teenagers showed even more vulnerability to cyclical changes. A 1-percent

99

decline in aggregate employment reduced nonwhite teenage employment by 5 percent. Also, during a recession a nonwhite adult male is 1.8 times as likely to lose his job as a white adult male.

However, if low-wage workers and teenagers are hurt most by an economic downswing, one might expect their employment levels to benefit most by an economic recovery. Using the example above, as the economy improves the teenage worker's productivity would increase to $3.00 an hour, and it would pay for a firm to employ this young worker. More teenagers might be fired during a recession; but, this model would seem to indicate that when the economy moves in the upward direction, a higher relative number of teenagers would be employed.

This would be true if the minimum wage rate were held at $2.90 an hour. But if, when times improve, the minimum wage is raised to, say, $3.10 an hour, employers would still find it unprofitable to hire teen-age workers. This, according to Kosters and Welch, happened during the 14 years they analyzed; repeated increases in the minimum wage ran ahead of teenagers' marginal productivity and discouraged employers from hiring them. Employment levels during recessions were lower, and few teenagers were employed even during boom periods because of the increasing level and coverage of minimum wages. The teenage share of normal employment, or long-term growth rates, was reduced, and the number of teenagers in the highly transitional part of the work force increased. Based on this model, it appears that minimum wage legislation has increased the responsiveness of teenage labor markets to cyclical patterns.

This conclusion is not without problems. Models that test for cyclical patterns due to minimum wages are highly dependent upon long-run trend measurements. However, various measures or estimation techniques of long-run trends produce different residuals. There are numerous ways to measure long-run trends, and there is no best method for all seasons. Moreover, placing workers in one—and only one—category is no less arbitrary. The Kosters-

Welch estimates found that during the period they investigated the size of the teenage population increased by 49 percent, while the size of the adult population showed a 14-percent growth rate. Kosters and Welch did not fully consider variables for demographic shifts, and there is no evidence that their results retain statistical significance when allowances are made for changes in the age composition of the labor force that occurred between 1954 and 1968.[13]

The third group of problems deals with investments in human capital by improving the education, training, and health care of the work force. A firm that has made a considerable investment in training a worker is less likely to lay off that worker in a recession than a worker who has received little if any training. Wide cyclical shifts in teenage employment and unemployment could be due in part to the fact that few firms have made significant investments in these young workers. Higher cyclical fluctuations in teenage and low-wage worker labor markets could be due to any number of factors, including the distribution of human capital investments, minimum wages, or other aggregate demand and supply forces. Reliable statistical techniques to measure the impact of these variables are still to be designed.

Lastly, one prime assumption of the cyclical model is that all workers are paid a wage equal to their marginal productivity. This might be viewed more as an assertion preached by traditional economists than as gospel truth that needs no proof to convince the faithful. Doubters may, however, be forgiven for questioning conclusions based on models that are the products of fertile imaginations, even if the theories have garnered the respectability that comes with age.

Job Rationing Models

When minimum wages were first proposed, critics made dire predictions about the consequences that would result should the government embark on such a foolhardy venture. The government did adopt the legislation, and the fact that the calamity could not be proved was blamed on the limited data and available tools. Clinging to the old faith, traditional economists hoped that computer technology and regression analysis would make the difference and reveal major negative impacts of placing a floor on wages. But the use of modern statistical techniques has not produced strikingly clear results. Only when certain assumptions are made, and other factors ignored, have minimum wages tended to show a highly significant major effect. Also, the studies have focused on teenage labor markets, almost ignoring adults.

More recently economists have focused on job rationing models, attempting to picture labor flows due to the minimum wage. Earlier research considered the different alternatives of employment, unemployment, school, military service, and other nonmarket activities available to youth, but the rationing models attempt to quantify the impact of minimum wages on the selection of options. The number of teenagers in school or in the military is assumed to be affected by the wage floor. Instead of examining only unemployment and employment data, a job rationing model may seek to investigate whether the elimination of the minimum wage would induce youths to leave school and enter the work force. It might analyze whether the number of potential job seekers who became discouraged and gave up seeking a job is due to the minimum wage. The impact of the minimum wage on the military establishment in attempting to meet manpower requirements could also be explored. The above are examples of the broad questions raised by the researchers. But a prime notion behind these models is that the minimum wage rations individuals—particularly youths—and blocks them from exercising the free choices they could make in competitive markets.

Illustrative of these efforts is a simple two-sector model constructed by Finis Welch.[14] Given the conditions in Figure 14 the wage rate in both the covered and uncovered sectors is W_0, with E_c

representing workers employed in the protected portion of the economy and E_u those in the uncovered sector. If the minimum wage rate is increased to W_1, only the wages in the covered sector will respond since the uncovered sector does not have to meet an FLSA wage order. But as wages in the covered sector rise to W_1, more people will seek the higher wages in this portion of the economy. Yet at an increased wage level employers in the covered sector will find labor more expensive. Hence, they will only want to employ E_1 workers. The demand for workers in the covered sector, given a wage rate of W_1, will be less than the supply of willing bodies. The result is the rationing of jobs.

Figure 14.   Job rationing models attempt to estimate the flow of workers between sectors of the economy due to the wage floor.

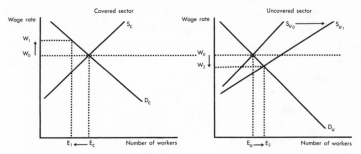

Workers unable to get a job in the protected sector will now either have to try to find work in the uncovered sector, withdraw from the labor force, or remain unemployed in the hope of obtaining a job in the covered sector. But as more workers try to find a job in the unprotected sector, the supply of labor to this low-wage portion of the economy will increase. (In Figure 14, the supply of labor in the uncovered sector moves out to the right from Su_0 to Su_1.) If the supply of labor in the sector not covered by the minimum wage increases, then the wage paid in this area will fall to W_2. The total impact of the minimum wage is now to increase the wages paid in the covered sector and at the same time decrease employment in this part of the economy. Meanwhile, minimum wages reduce the wage paid in the noncovered sector, and they also increase the number of low-paid workers employed in the unprotected jobs.

These types of models expand the horizons of minimum wage investigations beyond wage gains or job losses. Two factors are dominant: (1) the elasticity of demand for workers, which measures the relative responsiveness to prices or wages, and (2) the withdrawal rate of workers from the labor force. The higher the demand elasticity for labor in the covered sector, the greater will be the displacement of workers from the covered to the noncovered sector. If the responsiveness to wage increases is very high in the covered sector, then a large number of workers will find themselves displaced. As these displaced workers try to find work in the nonprotected sector, the elasticity of demand in this portion of the economy also plays a key role. The smaller the responsiveness to wages in the latter sector, the greater will be the decline in wages for people not protected by FLSA.

This model predicts that as the minimum wage rises, the fortunate workers will receive wage increases as others are forced out, taking lower wages or leaving the work force. The net result will depend in large measure upon withdrawal rates, the elasticity of demand in the covered sector, and the number of people who remain unemployed in an effort to land a job in the covered sector. Theory alone cannot predict what the net result will be, and the question remains an open empirical issue. Given one set of estimated values for these variables, the net effect will be an increase in average rates; a different set could show a decline. The point is that economic theory—all by itself—cannot even predict the direction of the shift.

Welch estimated that a 10-percent increase in the minimum wage could result in a 3-percent decline in the share of teenage employment. Based on simulation analysis, he suggested that if

FLSA coverage for teenagers was increased by 9 percentage points and the minimum wage was increased from 40 to 50 percent of the average wage paid in the manufacturing sector, then the ratio of teenage to adult employment would decline by 9 percent.

Withdrawal rates and elasticities play a crucial role, and yet supply responses often must be assumed. For example, Welch's estimates are grounded on simple assumptions about the supply of teenagers, including the decision of whether an individual will seek work or remain out of the labor force. But this is a complex decision influenced by many other factors besides minimum wages. It might be expected that alternative forms of income, such as welfare, food stamps, or added educational opportunities, would have a role in the propensity of people to seek work or remain outside of the labor force. These variables, as well as population shifts, are not directly considered in this analysis. As noted, workers not covered by federal minimum wage laws often receive some protection under various state laws. When state laws are also considered, an index of coverage and noncoverage can run into difficult estimation problems.

For the purpose of public policy the claim that some workers are better off because of minimum wages at the expense of other workers requires some realistic estimate about the quantities involved. If the lot of the majority improves, even at the expense of a minority, then the latter may be compensated by other measures. Programs might be designed to wash out the negative effects experienced by a relatively few workers, as in the case of trade adjustment legislation, which attempts to compensate the victims of imports.

The job rationing model also has been used to estimate the impact of the minimum wage on teenage employment. Welch estimated that significant negative employment results were experienced by teenagers in manufacturing and retail trade. Essentially no impact was found in the service industries. Contrary to expectations, the minimum wage appeared to have a positive influence in some industries—including wholesale trade, transportation and communication, real estate, finance, and insurance.

Beyond the specific estimates produced by job rationing models, the thrust of these investigations represents a theoretical shift. Since the start of the minimum wage programs, a middle-ground position viewed minimum wages as a tradeoff that would produce benefits as well as costs. Job rationing models attempt to examine the nature of this tradeoff in which some people are helped while others are made worse off. Even if the minimum wage does create some unemployment, it does not necessarily justify condemnation of the entire wage floor. The cost must be compared with the benefits, which might include some income redistribution or a reduction in the number of the working poor. Other analysts have used this type of job rationing model as a starting point for their evaluation of minimum wages. There have been attempts to make the models more realistic and to derive estimates based on less rigid assumptions. But the introduction of this structure means that a growing number of analysts have entered the middle-ground position and have ceased to view the wage floor as either an unmitigated evil or an almost costless blessing.

Jacob Mincer tried to use a job rationing model that did not assume only one direction of labor flow.[15] Prior models had tended to assume that increases in the minimum wage predetermined the direction of labor flows. If the minimum wage was increased by, say, 25 percent, then the flow of labor would be to the uncovered portion of the economy as the higher wage floor decreased the number of jobs in the covered sector. However, Mincer pointed out that the direction of the net labor flow, or mobility, is an open empirical question. For example, a higher minimum wage might result in a flow of labor to the uncovered sector, but it might also encourage more workers in the unprotected part of the economy to seek better jobs in the covered portion of the economy. Given unemployment insurance benefits and other public and private forms of income support, workers might remain unemployed for a while in the hopes that a higher paying job in the covered sector will become available.

A lower minimum wage might increase the number of jobs open to young workers, and this might reduce the percentage of teenagers in school. But a lower minimum wage might have the opposite effect. With lower wages, more teenagers might opt for longer education rather than full-time employment. Mincer suggested that the direction of the flow would depend upon the vacancy rate in the covered sector, the degree of minimum wage coverage, and the supply and demand elasticities. In his job rationing model the flow of labor could be in any direction instead of along some predetermined path. He estimated that the impact of minimum wage did not appear to be statistically significant for males between the ages of 25 and 64, nonwhite males 65 years or older, or nonwhite females 20 years and older. The negative results were strongest for nonwhite teenagers, followed by nonwhite males between the ages of 20 and 24. Minimum wages also had some minor impact on nonwhite males aged 25 to 64. Holding all other factors constant, increases in minimum wages tended to decrease the size of the labor force.

Job rationing models have been expanded to include some demographic changes and shifts in labor force participation rates. Considering these factors, James F. Regan, Jr., estimated that youth employment in 1972 would have been 3.8 percent higher in the absence of the 1966 amendments to the FLSA (which raised the minimum and extended coverage) resulting in an increased unemployment rate of about the same magnitude.[16] Martin Feldstein concluded that the wage floor not only blocks unqualified, or low productivity, youth from landing jobs, but it also hurts teenagers who are willing to purchase training in the form of lower wages.[17] J. Wilson Mixon, Jr., estimated that the minimum wage inhibits the rate of quitting in low-wage industries.[18]

The last three mentioned studies indicate a basic problem with statistical analysis. Even if the estimated numbers in all three

107

studies were correct, different conclusions could be drawn from the same data. Mixon states that because the minimum wage inhibits the quit rate in low-wage industries, the wage floor reduces the dynamic market efficiency in these sectors. The minimum wage reduces the economic incentives to change jobs, and for this reason the wage floor is producing a negative impact. However, even if one assumes that Mixon's estimated numbers are correct, a far different interpretation could explain his findings. It may be that the minimum wage is reducing some of the differences between primary and secondary labor markets and that, if given some protection, low-wage workers will behave a bit more like workers in the higher-paid sectors. A lower quit rate indicates that the minimum wage produces more stable employment patterns. Instead of showing negative results, Mixon's estimates seem to be outlining several positive benefits resulting from the FLSA.

Regan has estimated one cost of the minimum wage, but he ignored the benefits. The estimated 3.8-percent reduction in employment might be more than compensated for by the salutary impacts of minimum wages. Feldstein assumes that in a free market teenage workers will wind up in jobs that provide worthwhile training. However, the reality is that young workers often can land only dead-end jobs, such as in the fast-food industry, which do not provide training leading to better jobs. Not only do value judgments enter into the statistical estimation process, but they also influence a researcher in drawing conclusions from data. What the estimated numbers seem to be saying often depends on one's preconceived notions and biases.

Income Effects of Minimum Wages

Granted the costs created by minimum wages, are they worth paying? If minimum wages involve a tradeoff, then one must also consider the benefits, which might include higher wages for some workers and the reduction of poverty. The FLSA was designed to affect incomes, but it has only been since the mid-1970s that economists have aimed their statistical guns at these basic income issues.

A major goal of minimum wage legislation has been to provide a basic level of income or a minimum standard of living for working Americans. Compared with numerous studies on the employment and unemployment aspects of minimum wages, there has been only scant attention to income effects. But until the mid-1970s the data did not exist to explore the effectiveness of minimum wages in ameliorating poverty, the prevalence of low-wage workers in low-income families, and the impact of minimum wages on income distribution. Such information is essential to assess whether the costs produced by the wage floor are worth paying.

Lacking data to answer these questions directly, a few analysts have tried speculation and conceptualization. For example, Albert Zucker noted that the elasticity of demand for labor also provides clues about the aggregate size of the wage bill paid to labor.[19] If the elasticity is less than 1 (i.e., the demand for labor is not very responsive to wage changes), then as the wage rates increase the wage bill rises and labor as a group will have a higher income. However, if the elasticity is greater than 1 (i.e., the demand for labor is highly responsive to the wage rate), then as the wage rate rises the wage bill will go down and labor as a group will have a lower income. At unit elasticity there will be no change in the wage bill as the wage rate increases—labor as a group will not experience any change in their income level.

Zucker's regression estimates for 1947 to 1966 indicated that the long-run demand elasticities for production workers are in essence unity: higher wages received by some workers will be matched by curtailment of wages paid to others or by reduction of the number of workers. If Zucker's estimates are correct, it would mean that the minimum wage would have some distributional

109

effects but a very small impact on total labor income. Workers who retain their jobs will be paid more, but the total wage bill will remain virtually unchanged because some workers will be fired.

These conclusions were based in large measure on economic theory and were not tested by income data. Also, the conclusions are based on aggregates, and what might be true for the whole could be false for many of its parts. With the recent expansions in data bases, researchers have been able to extend their range of analysis. In May 1973 the government's Current Population Survey (CPS) added an annual supplement that collected data on earnings. These data are to be expanded on a quarterly basis. In addition, a CPS supplement conducted each March has collected information on annual family income since 1967.

These data sources provide a link between wage rates and family income, which can help an analyst in attempting to answer questions concerning minimum wages and poverty. Interestingly enough, the Bureau of Labor Statistics has not conducted minimum wage studies linking the wage and income data, and so the task has fallen to several private researchers. The combined data sets and the link-up are not pure or simple—they never are. The May survey collects current wage rates of individuals; the March survey collects data on family income during the previous year. Terence Kelly and Edward Gramlich have used the new data to study minimum wages and family incomes.

Poverty and Minimum Wages

Kelly has tried to estimate the extent to which a boost in the minimum wage reduces poverty. Based on March and May labor force data, he simulated the net effects of changes in the minimum wage. This is a difficult task, and Kelly placed a clear *caveat emptor* sign on his findings by indicating that his efforts represent first approximations rather than conclusions.[20] The shortcomings to which he refers are well worth examining.

First, the simulation considers only the direct effect of minimum wage changes and ignores all secondary effects. A higher minimum wage could increase the wages of workers paid slightly more than the minimum as firms and employers attempt to keep existing wage differentials. Also, contrary to job rationing models, the minimum wage may indirectly increase the wages of workers in noncovered industries. An increased wage floor could shift the entire wage distribution upward. Second, given the limitations of applying simulation techniques, the model did not consider the employment effects of minimum wages. Third, changes in minimum wages, which affect family incomes, should have an influence on government transfer payments, (i.e., income support programs). However, these changes are also ignored in the model. Fourth, the expanded in-kind income, such as the value of food stamps or housing subsidies, is not measured by the CPS. Fifth, to generate estimates the researcher was required to make simple assumptions about the extent of FLSA coverage and compliance.

Kelly used the May 1974 sample supplement to obtain observations on current wage rates and the March 1974 supplement for family income levels. There is a problem, however, since the March 1974 survey reported 1973 income levels. The CPS is a stratified random sample of households picked to reflect the composition of the entire population. A household that is picked remains in the sample for four consecutive months, is dropped from the sample for the next eight months, and then is placed back in the sample for the same four months during the next year, leaving, at best, about 50 percent of the households that are in the March CPS in the May survey. But in reality some households, for various reasons, do not participate in both surveys; a household that reported in March might have moved or be otherwise unavailable by May when the enumerator comes to collect the data, or a family could refuse to give some information. Many of the observations had to be excluded from the simulation estimates because numerous households had incomplete or missing data records. In

111

fact, 33 percent of the sampled households did not report wage rate data in the May survey. Other household observations had to be excluded because the data from March could not be matched with information contained in the May CPS. In the end Kelly wound up with a sample consisting of 12,409 households (about half of the theoretical 50 percent), including 1,816—or 14.6 percent—living in poverty.

Given the data on these 1,816 households, Kelly estimated the number of families that would have been lifted out of poverty at different levels of the minimum wage. He assumed complete coverage and compliance with the FLSA, as follows:

Wage rate	Poor families (number)	Poverty reduction as a result of the minimum wage (percent)
Initial position	1,816	—
Assumed minimum wage		
$1.60	1,789	1.5
$2.00	1,770	2.5
$2.50	1,731	4.7
$2.65	1,712	5.8
$2.85	1,694	6.7
$3.50	1,639	9.7

Kelly considered these estimates to be amazingly small. To reduce the number of families in poverty by about 10 percent, the minimum wage would have to be increased by almost 119 percent. However, there are several problems that make it risky to extrapolate results based on a sample of this size. The matched sample observations may not be a true random sample of the whole U.S. population, and this could bias the estimates. Even if the May and March CPS samples were random and unbiased, the way this subsample of families was produced could prejudice the results.

These estimates point out that just became a person earns a low wage, it does not mean that the worker is also a member of a family in poverty. A teenage worker may be paid the minimum wage while working during the summer months, but the teenager's parents could be well-paid business executives. The reverse could also be true. Just because a person is paid a wage above the minimum, it does not mean that the worker's family is out of poverty. The person may be the sole supporter of a large family and may work only intermittently.

Kelly suggested that his findings were tentative, but they may have brought into question the effectiveness of the minimum wage as an income transfer device designed to fight poverty. There are always problems associated with programs designed to aid the poor; yet the question is, Are the problems so large that they warrant junking the entire program? Minimum wages will help some families who are not in poverty. Whether this is a sound public policy is open to dispute.

Analysts should consider that every bit of income helps working poor families, even if they are not pulled over some statistical poverty line. Suppose a family of four had earnings of $4,784 (i.e., 2,080 hours of work at a minimum wage of $2.30). When the minimum wage is increased to $2.65, this family will have an annual income of $5,512. Since the poverty line is $6,200, Kelly's model would show that the minimum wage had not lifted this family out of destitution. This is true, but the family's income still is $728 higher with the increase in the wage floor. This improvement produced by the minimum wage will not be captured in a simulation that uses only a rigid benchmark. Higher wages provide an added incentive to seek work. In a society that asserts that the work ethic is a sound principle, the minimum wage may still produce social benefits even if some of the benefits are garnered by families that are above the poverty level.

In an effort to solve some of these rigid benchmark problems, Kelly also used a *poverty gap* measure to estimate the income gains to the poor who remain below the official destitution index even when the minimum wage is increased. The poverty gap is a measure of the amount by which total reported family income falls short of the poverty threshold. One hypothesis is that as the minimum wage is increased the poverty gap will be reduced. Kelly found this to be the case, and his results showed the following:

Wage rate	Poverty gap	Poverty gap reduction as a result of the minimum wage (percent)
Initial position	$2,170,999	——
Assumed minimum wage		
$1.60	$2,135,731	1.6
$2.00	$2,114,239	2.6
$2.50	$2,061,207	5.1
$2.65	$2,044,511	5.8
$2.85	$2,025,313	6.7
$3.50	$1,971,448	9.2

Even though the wage floor reduced the poverty gap, he felt the estimated results were small. The minimum wage would have to be more than doubled to reduce the poverty gap by 9 percent.

If the minimum wage were the only tool used in fighting poverty, then this estimate would indicate that hefty boosts would be required to reduce destitution in America. But minimum wages are not the only tool to fight poverty, nor were they ever designed to be the sole tool. Minimum wages are one of several programs used in a policy mix in an attempt to alleviate these problems. It serves no purpose to compare minimum wages with only idealistic and theoretical alternatives. "Small" is a relative concept. If these estimates are correct, then increasing the minimum wage from $2.90 to $3.12 would lift about one-quarter of a million Americans out of poverty. How one views this tradeoff cannot be disentangled from basic value judgments. Minimum wages might not have produced dramatic changes within our society. But one might question whether—if they had the result of causing dramatic, radical change—they would ever have been passed by Congress.

Who Is Better Off?

Most minimum wage research has centered on only one narrow aspect of the wage floor, and the resulting judgments have tended to reflect this constraint. In recent years economists have broadened their econometric vista and have attempted to estimate the costs in relation to the benefits. Increased information on wages and family income is one factor that made this shift in research methods possible, but the explicit assumption that the minimum wage involves a tradeoff also has provided an important ideological change in outlook.

Edward Gramlich designed an ambitious model with which he tried to determine the beneficiaries and victims of the minimum wage.[21] The model is necessarily complex; yet it raises the hard choice faced by a low-wage worker who is offered the opportunity of a minimum wage but at the risk of losing a job. In a sense this minimum wage offer is like any bet, and the odds associated with the gamble could influence the worker's decision. But in a mature welfare state the minimum wage bet must consider the level and availability of income supports. If the latter are generous, then the degree of hardship experienced because of being unemployed is reduced. If there were not transfer payments and the alternatives were to work or to starve, then the prospect of being unemployed might appear to be dire. Hence, income support programs influence a worker's reaction to the minimum wage bet. Also, the mean duration of employment and unemployment spells would influence the terms of the bet. The welfare regulations would also have a different effect on different groups. For example, assistance might be offered only to females and not to males.

Tradeoff models require estimates for the probability of being paid a higher wage in the covered sector of the economy, the impact of transfer payments, the duration of unemployment for subgroups in the labor markets, and labor turnover rates. Given

115

these factors, the elasticities of demand for labor play a key role in determining how different people would rationally react to the minimum wage gamble. A low elasticity of demand for labor involves little chance of losing a job when the minimum wage is increased; a rising elasticity increases the probability of unemployment, raising the costs of minimum wages.

Model builders in a sense work the problem backwards. They first consider the value of a number of variables, including the level of transfer payments, the duration of unemployment spells, and minimum wage income effects. Given these estimates, they then attempt to measure the elasticity of demand for each group to determine the break-even point, at which the group would be neither better nor worse off as a result of the wage floor.

Once these break-even elasticities are determined, the job is to estimate the actual elasticities for the various groups. If the actual elasticity for a group is less than its break-even figure, then the odds of the minimum wage bet are assumed to be quite good. However, if the actual elasticity is greater than the break-even figure, the minimum wage bet is judged as not being a good deal for this group of workers.

Using this model, Gramlich estimated that adult female workers, as a group, were the main beneficiaries of statutory minimum wages. The employment effects were small and could not even come close to washing out the benefits received by adult women because of the minimum wage. Also, the model showed that minimum wages resulted in no significant substitution of part-time work for full-time employment as far as women were concerned. The results were so positive for adult females that Gramlich was led to question, "Can it be that George Meany is really a feminist?"[22]

Adult males also appear to benefit from an increase in minimum wages. But the actual elasticities for adult men were much closer to the break-even level than for adult females. There was also a noticeable increase in part-time employment for adult men. One part of the minimum wage bet for this group may be the increased probability of finding only part-time work.

For teenagers the employment elasticity was below the break-even range, and Gramlich noted that teenagers appear to be better off after an increase in the minimum wage. However, there are other results in teenage labor markets that cause this first appearance to lose a good deal of its luster. The wage floor does seem to decrease the chances of full-time teenage employment, forcing more young workers into part-time employment. Only when the elasticities of both part-time and full-time employment are combined do minimum wages appear to benefit teenagers. Being forced into part-time employment and denied full-time jobs could produce lasting effects on a teenager's worklife advancement and income. On the basis of these estimates, Gramlich favors a subminimum wage for teenage workers. Recognizing that being a low-wage worker is not synonymous with living below the poverty threshold, Gramlich found demographic differences. For adult workers the correlation between low wages and low family income is quite strong, even if it is not perfect. In 1972, nonetheless, 12 percent of low-wage adult workers were members of families with incomes over $15,000, compared with a median family income of roughly $11,000. This would indicate that as the minimum wage is increased there are some spillover benefits that go to relatively high-income families. Yet for teenagers this spillover effect is larger. About 40 percent of low-wage teenagers were in families with incomes above $15,000.

Since the correlation between individual wages and family income is far from perfect, the minimum wage will have only a restricted impact on income redistribution. Gramlich estimated that when the minimum wage increases the income paid to low-wage workers by $1 billion, adult workers will receive about $0.7 billion. But of this $0.7 billion, 25 percent will go to families that already have incomes above the median.

Tradeoff models show that the minimum wage produces some job loss for adult workers. But it is less than the wage gains obtained by this group under minimum wages. On balance, adult workers appear to be made better off by the wage floor. The opportunities for teenagers of finding full-time employment are reduced, and younger workers may be shunted into part-time work when they seek full-time employment. As a result of both spillover effects and the relatively small size of minimum wage increases, wage floor programs by themselves have not produced dramatic or radical changes in income distribution patterns.

Future Directions

Econometric studies have enabled researchers to broaden their investigations on the impacts of minimum wages and to weigh and analyze the various tradeoffs involved. Nonetheless, the available tools still remain inadequate to measure the effects of minimum wages, and the conclusions reached depend as ever on doubtful assumptions and educated guesses. The computer can speed up calculations; but it is no substitute for judgment, and by itself the machine can not generate insights. The numerous investigations and countless computer simulations have yielded only very rough first approximations about the impact of minimum wages. Judged from the findings concerning minimum wages, social scientists have a long way to go before they will enter the statistical golden age envisioned by Stigler. Estimates about the impacts of minimum wages vary so much that they often are of limited use to the policymaker.

The predictions of dire harm to the economy have not been borne out by repeated statistical investigations. Neither does the notion that the minimum wage is an almost costless benefit appear to hold up under scrutiny. But considering the tendency of wage rates to cluster at the minimum for large sections of the labor force, many workers enjoy an improved standard of living due to the FLSA, even if some jobs have been eliminated. However, quantification of this tradeoff remains elusive. The estimates and predictions still hinge on many restrictive and simplistic assumptions and biases, rarely explicitly stated. One major trend for future research probably will be to generate more accurate estimates that require assumptions based on empirical data rather than on the ideologies of the researchers.

A priority item on the agenda of investigators interested in the income effects of minimum wages is to explore in greater depth the nexus of statutory minimum wages with work and welfare issues. Given that American society still blesses the work ethic, the need is to investigate how strong a work incentive is created by the wage floor. A related issue is the link between programs designed to induce work and their effectiveness in counteracting the negative employment effects produced by minimum wages. There is also a need to illuminate the relationship between minimum wages and other programs to reduce destitution.

The best that can be said for the model builders is that they have raised intriguing questions. In the process they have whetted the appetites of policymakers and analysts for more knowledge. But to raise questions does not mean that one has answered them. In common with similar efforts, the model may stimulate speculation or exalt the minds of economists, but the data required to assess the model often do not exist or are very difficult to obtain. The models—to borrow from the late Jacob Viner—lack vital organs. As a consequence, to apply these elegant models to the real world the econometrician is forced to make rigid and heroic assumptions. In the process not only the utility of the model is lost but also its elegance. Too frequently the econometrician, like the emperor of old, is found under close scrutiny to be naked.

Economic research has not made the crucial quantitative leap outlined by Lord Kelvin. At best, all the models and research have succeeded in offering only very rough first approximations of the impact of minimum wages; the policymaker is left to base decisions in large part on gut reactions and normative judgments.

5

Policy Options—The 1977 Round

The Dual Goals

In order to improve the lot of the working poor, Congress has established a dual but sometimes conflicting set of goals aimed at increasing the wages and income paid to the working poor but without significantly destroying job opportunities. This is a tall order, requiring the determination of the specific level at which the wage floor will be built. Other thorny issues facing policymakers are the extent of coverage and whether the same level will apply for all workers. A subminimum wage for youths has been proposed to make up for the presumed lower productivity of teenagers as compared with that of experienced workers. Similarly, differences in cost of living among regions and between rural and metropolitan areas have generated proposals to establish minimum wage differentials that would reflect area variations. The desirability of exempting handicapped workers must also be weighed.

There is also the question of how often the wage floor should be reviewed. Minimum wages are currently established by a process of periodic amendments to the FLSA. An alternative approach would be to index the minimum wage so that it will automatically move in tandem with an appropriate statistical time series. The most often mentioned approach is to peg the wage floor to some percentage index of the average hourly earnings in the manufacturing sector. Finally, policymakers must also consider the potential inflationary impact of increasing the minimum wage.

Yet the goals, as outlined in the original minimum wage legislation, can not be considered in isolation from other government programs designed to ameliorate poverty among the working poor. How does, or should, the minimum wage tie in with the government's massive system of transfer payments? What part, if any, can minimum wages play in the drive for welfare reform?

The 1977 round of congressional amendments to the FLSA provides an excellent case study of how lawmakers have tried to cope with these issues. It shows the politics behind minimum wage decisions and the uses—and no less frequently, alas, the abuses—of economic evidence. As the summary of results produced by econometric studies indicates, minimum wage policy decisions are as much an art as a science. By reviewing the specific issues, the latest congressional round shows the complexity and difficulties in reaching consensus on wage floor policy options. As usual the 1977 round was no exception, leaving many of the key issues unresolved. To help Congress with the next round of amendments, the lawmakers have created the federal Minimum Wage Study Commission to explore the gamut of wage floor issues.

The Issues

Congressional action on fixing the specific level of the wage floor has fallen into a general pattern. With the dual objectives of providing higher income for the working poor but avoiding major job losses, Congress has tended to set the wage floor at about 50 percent of the average hourly rate paid in the manufacturing sector. There is no firm scientific reason behind this pattern. It is based more on a hunch, or educated guess, that at this relative level the minimum wage will be reasonable and accomplish both main objectives. However, as the years pass, inflationary trends and rising real wages reduce the relative degree of protection afforded by the wage floor. At a fixed dollar level, the minimum wage over a period of time represents far less than 50 percent of the average paid to manufacturing workers. The result is a new round of congressional amendments boosting the minimum wage back to about the same real level of protection for low-wage workers.

Pegging the Wage Floor

During the 1977 round pro-minimum-wage forces tried to end this historical pattern of minimum wage setting by first increasing the wage floor to a higher relative rate than in most of the previous rounds. Second, they proposed to index the wage floor so that adjustments would be automatic instead of requiring periodic congressional attention. This was in line with the growing trend to tie wages and benefits paid by government programs, including social security and welfare payments, to changes in the cost of living. In the private sector a growing number of union contracts provide for the adjustments of wage rates in conformity with changes in the consumer price index. The campaign to index the minimum wage is another example of attempting to adjust the level of wages automatically instead of waiting for the legislative process to make the changes.

Organized labor proposed an immediate increase of the minimum wage to $3 an hour, a 30-percent hike in the wage floor. On top of that, the AFL-CIO called for an automatic mechanism to be built into the law to hold the minimum wage at 60 percent of the average hourly earnings in the manufacturig sector. While labor leaders noted that they believed other improvements should be made in the FLSA, they insisted that they were holding their demands to "bread and butter issues of wages and jobs."[1] As AFL-CIO president George Meany put it, this proposal would bring

122

low-wage workers and their families above the federal government's official poverty level. In February 1977 the chairman of the
House Subcommittee on Labor Standards, John H. Dent of Pennsylvania, introduced H.R. 3744, which contained most of organized labor's wishes.

Despite the persistent economic research on minimum wages,
the art of politics has a far greater bearing on the ultimate decisions concerning the wage floor formulated by policymakers.
During the 1976 presidential primaries candidate Jimmy Carter
was hardly the first choice of either organized labor or many of the
traditionally liberal groups of the Democratic party. Yet, given the
choice between President Ford and Jimmy Carter, labor worked
hard for the Democratic candidate. However, because they
hopped onto the bandwagon late, the Carter administration did not
feel as beholden to regular power blocs within the party as past
Democratic administrations had felt. One result was a White
House minimum wage package significantly less than what
organized labor had hoped for.

The Dent subcommittee held hearings on the bill in March
1977. The Carter administration indicated that it was sympathetic
to the goals outlined in the Dent bill, but concerns over inflation
and unemployment levels led the administration to present a
separate, and more modest, package of its own. As outlined at the
hearings by Secretary of Labor Ray Marshall, the administration
suggested a flat minimum wage increase of about 8.7 percent to
$2.50 an hour and indexation to be fixed at 50 percent of straight-
time hourly earnings of production and nonsupervisory workers in
manufacturing. Besides a smaller percentage figure, the administration's proposed index would have used a lower base figure for
the adjustment process; overtime pay is included in gross hourly
earnings figures but not in straight-time hourly earnings data. In
recent years the difference between the two levels has been close to
4 percent. Neither the Carter nor the Dent index proposal included
the value of fringe benefits in its formula.

123

Since indexing would represent a major departure from previous methods of adjusting the minimum wage, Marshall suggested that the Department of Labor study indexing as part of its annual minimum wage report to Congress. The report would consider whether the indexing formula was working as expected, whether it had increased the sensitivity of wages to past inflationary experiences, and whether indexing had changed the wage-setting process in many labor markets.

Within the administration Marshall had advocated a higher minimum wage package but was overruled. During the hearings he expressed a hope that the administration could "achieve a reasonable reconciliation" on these issues.[2] Organized labor's reaction to the Carter package was both swift and strong. George Meany called it "shameful" and disturbing for those who looked to the new administration for economic and social justice.[3] The Coalition for a Fair Minimum Wage—composed of over 100 labor, civil rights, civic, and religious groups—also denounced the administration's proposal since it would leave many workers below the federal poverty income guidelines. The coalition argued that an increase of 53 cents an hour would be needed just to restore the buying power lost because of inflation since 1974. The group distributed over 2 million post cards to be returned to members of Congress and the White House urging support for the higher levels.[4]

Potential Winners and Losers

However, other interest groups were tugging on Congress in a different direction. The Chamber of Commerce of the United States warned that the economic consequences of the Dent bill would be the elimination of over 2 million full- and part-time jobs in the private sector. Consumer prices, as a result of this legislation, would increase by roughly 3 percent. Jack Carlson, vice president and chief economist of the Chamber of Commerce, proposed that

Congress delay consideration of minimum wage legislation for two years until the economy more fully recovered. Then if 5-percent unemployment were achieved, some amendments might be in order. Carlson also advocated a significant differential in the minimum wages for youths.[5]

Lawmakers were mindful of the unemployment impact that might result from a boost in the minimum wage. But the 2 million figure was a rather dramatic number, and it was cited in many media reports on the legislation. The Chamber of Commerce also pinpointed the potential victims of the increase proposed by Congressman Dent. Small business firms would experience a 6.4–percent increase in labor costs as a result of the proposed measure, and they would be forced to raise prices by 5.5 percent. Teenagers would lose 952,000 jobs, workers aged 20 to 24 would lose 610,000 jobs, and workers over 55 years old would lose 497,000 jobs. The chamber also estimated that nonwhites would experience a 533,000 job loss, while female workers could count on 439,000 fewer jobs. However, the chamber estimated that 364,000 jobs could be preserved if employers were allowed to employ youths aged 16 to 18 at 85 percent of the regular minimum wage and that 617,000 jobs in this age group would be saved if the differential was 75 percent of the adult minimum. Besides national estimates, the chamber set out comparable figures for states and each of the nation's 435 congressional districts, and copies of the dire predictions and other materials were sent to all members of Congress.

Given the magnitude and precision of the Chamber of Commerce estimates, it is important to investigate how these numbers were derived. The chamber indicated that the aforementioned Gramlich and Mincer studies were the foundation upon which its estimates were based. It appears that the chamber relied upon Mincer's estimates of elasticities and relative employment impact, which were on the high side in comparison with other econometric studies. However, even Mincer's computer simulations did not

125

produce numbers as large as the chamber estimates; the basic Mincer coefficient estimates were "updated" for the chamber by three University of Chicago economists.[6] The basis for the chamber's inflation estimates were no less subject to doubt. Mincer's study did not have any inflation figures, and Gramlich noted that the chamber's inflation estimates were much too high if they were based on his work.[7]

The chamber estimates probably received the greatest media attention, but Congress turned to other econometric evidence provided by the dismal science. Several of the researchers cited in Chapters 3 and 4 testified before House and Senate committees on minimum wages, and they made a valiant effort to translate their findings into simple and clear English. In language understandable to members of Congress, Gramlich testified that his research had led him to a "kind of middle-of-the-road stance."[8] Minimum wages can be viewed as a tradeoff that creates some disemployment, but they also provide higher income to many low-wage workers. Concerning inflation, Gramlich estimated that the passage of the Dent bill would have boosted the price level by 1.3 percent. On balance, he opined, the size of the increase proposed by the Dent bill was too high.

Secretary Marshall told the lawmakers that the job loss would be about 90,000—or only roughly 5 percent of the Chamber of Commerce estimate. However, the Labor Department also used the Mincer and Gramlich studies in forming its job loss estimate. Clearly, econometric results, like Holy Scripture, can be cited by believers of different persuasions.

Numerous representatives of employers viewed with alarm the proposed boost in the minimum wage. One business executive contended that the Dent bill in less than one year would cause a direct wage cost increase of 159 percent for employees who receive at least 50 percent of their wages in tips. Being in the hotel business, he claimed that sales generated by employees in manufacturing were nearly three times those for the lodging industry.

Hotels could not generate the productivity increases to keep up with an index based on manufacturing unless the prices for accommodations and other hotel services were increased by 75 percent. These price increases would not be sustained in the marketplace, and occupancy rates at hotels and motels would fall. An index based on manufacturing wages would play havoc with the hotel service sector.

The president of the Women's Lobby defended the boost. She stated that most women sought employment because of economic necessity, and not for pin money. Close to 70 percent of the women who work either are single, widowed, divorced, or separated or have husbands who earn under $10,000 a year. Since women represent about 40 percent of the work force, and since females have a lower average wage than males, a higher relative number of women are directly affected by minimum wage legislation than men. With increasing family breakups, a growing number of young women are winding up as heads of households. If work is to be a realistic alternative to welfare, then a higher minimum wage is required.

Business, labor, and minority rights groups opposed the Carter administration package, and the votes to pass the Dent bill appeared to be lacking. Dent himself told supporters of the bill that he was not optimistic about the legislation's chances, given the combination of conservative opposition in Congress and the White House's position on the issue.

The Compromise

The bill remained stalled in the House Subcommittee on Labor Standards, and lawmakers as well as the White House were subjected to intensive lobbying. This, of course, is not unusual when Congress considers minimum wage legislation. But this time there seemed to be an added incentive. Early in the 1977 session—and much to organized labor's surprise—the common situs picketing bill went down to defeat. As an indication of this jolt to the Washington lobbying scene, the day after the vote the head of one of the largest business trade associations in the country exhorted his troops that if an extra hard effort were made, all pro-labor legislation could be defeated in the 95th Congress—including the Dent bill and labor law reform.

Tension between the White House and the AFL-CIO mounted when presidential advisor Hamilton Jordan stepped into the breach and urged the Carter administration to seek a compromise with the AFL-CIO on organized labor's legislative proposals. Early in June the president met with the leaders of the Coalition for a Fair Minimum Wage for an exchange of views.[9]

By mid-June the White House and the pro-minimum-wage forces had reached a compromise that would boost the minimum wage by roughly 15 percent to $2.65 an hour starting in January 1978. This represented approximately 51 percent of average straight-time hourly earnings of production and nonsupervisory workers in manufacturing. The minimum wage would then be indexed to 52 percent of this time series in January 1979 and 53 percent a year later, where it would be pegged thereafter.

Dent revised his bill to reflect the White House compromise, and the committee majority accepted the new bill 29 to 7.[10] The last amendment to the FLSA had been repealed by inflation, the majority asserted. Also, while black workers account for 11 percent of all workers covered by FLSA, they represent about 17 percent of those at the minimum wage. Only about 6 percent of the workers covered by FLSA were paid the minimum or less, and two out of three included in this group were women. For these reasons, a minimum wage increase was required to aid minority and female workers. Responding to the charges that the boost was excessive, the committee majority noted that the increases would have to be doubled to raise families out of poverty (given the usual assumptions of an urban family of four). Since the 1974 amendments straight-time average hourly earnings in manufacturing had increased by 28 percent in three years. Just to keep the minimum wage in line, or at the same relative level as in 1974, would have required a minimum wage of $2.94 an hour. Also, even with an index at 53 percent of manufacturing wages, covered workers being paid the minimum were not expected to reach poverty level income standards until 1984. If inflation were to heat up and manufacturing wages not keep pace, this goal would not even be reached by 1984. Given these factors, the proposed increase in the minimum was viewed as a moderate move.[11]

Concerning the inflationary impact of the bill, the majority asserted that there was a very weak link—if any—between minimum wages and inflation. The possibility that a mandated cost increase from Congress might be a contributing factor for keeping inflation going once the wage-price spiral has started was not fully considered by the committee in its report on the minimum wage legislation. The so-called ripple effect on existing wage structures was dismissed by the unsupported claim that only a very small bumping effect takes place when the wage floor is raised.

In a similar fashion, the majority of the committee denied any unemployment effects of minimum wage increases. Citing Department of Labor reports going back to 1950, the majority declared that "increases in the minimum wage rate do not adversely affect employment. In fact, subsequent to the 1949, 1961, 1967–68 minimum wage increases, unemployment actually decreased, and in 1965 unemployment remained unchanged."[12] The majority went to great lengths to refute the findings of the Chamber of Commerce that millions of people would be made jobless by the bill. However, the committee report was silent about other studies that differed from the conclusions reached by the government analysts. The majority also argued that a higher minimum was required to make employment a realistic alternative to welfare for low-wage workers. A low minimum wage was also called a subsidy to busi-

129

ness at the expense of both workers and the general public. Firms may profit from low wages by shifting the burden of providing a basic subsistence level to public institutions and private charity.[13]

The minority countered by insisting that studies of minimum wages had established a negative link between minimum wages and employment opportunities, glossing over in the heat of debate the investigators' reservations and assumptions and accepting their tentative conclusions as gospel truth. In fairness to Congress it must be acknowledged that some of the scholarly investigators, while testifying before the committee, oversold their findings. Also forgotten was the fact that the studies that have found a negative impact have tended to deal only with teenage labor markets. Extending these findings to adult labor markets may be highly misleading and incorrect. In fact, most studies in the area have cautioned about data limitations and the fact that only teenage labor markets were considered.

A second approach taken by critics of the proposal was to argue that the timing was poor. During a period of recovery from the worst recession since the 1930s, sizable minimum wage increases should not be made law lest the higher wages impede economic recovery. Cost-push inflation could also heat up due in part to boosting the wage floor. Minimum wages were not viewed as a prime source of price increases, but every little bit of government-regulated price hikes hurts. The difference in estimates by economists was noted, and some critics suggested that Congress hold off on any major minimum wage changes until a special commission had a chance to review the situation and report its findings to the lawmakers.

Indexing

A majority of the House Education and Labor Committee favored the addition of indexing as an integral part of the wage floor, holding that the working poor should not await the findings of a commission while watching the erosion of their meager incomes. Not only low-paid employees, but also their employers, according to this view, would benefit from a stable and regular pattern of change in the minimum wage. Both workers and business executives could anticipate and plan for the increases.

The majority viewed the periodical legislative review as unproductive use of congressional time and effort, delaying necessary action, not to mention creating frustrations for low-paid workers. FLSA amendments have tended to be deals negotiated amid intense pressure from various interest groups. Indexation was viewed as a way to rationalize the process, and Congress would not have to act to restore the real value of prior benefits that have been reduced by inflation.

Using hourly earnings in manufacturing for the index was viewed as superior to several other alternatives. Adjusting the minimum wage merely to maintain its purchasing power, the advocates of indexation argued, would prevent low-paid workers from sharing in the use of societal productivity to which the low-paid workers contribute. Tying minimum wage rates to increases only in the cost of living would defeat the very purpose of indexing the wage floor—to protect the earnings of low-wage workers not only from inflation but also in relation to those of more highly paid individuals. If the minimum wage had been adjusted to changes in cost of living since its inception in 1938, the wage floor would have been only about 55 percent of its 1977 level.

An alternative option is to tie the minimum wage to the poverty index, if the goal is to give low-wage workers income levels that pull their families out of poverty. A major problem of indexing the wage floor to the poverty level is that the minimum wage would require payments based on family size and needs. But as long as the wage structure for the rest of the economy does not consider worker needs in fixing compensation levels, a minimum wage adjusted for family size would be totally unpractical. It would be a case of the tail wagging the dog.

The most suitable minimum wage index is some percentage of average hourly wages. Such an index would protect the relative standing of minimum wage workers compared to others in the labor market. The House committee agreed with Secretary of Labor Marshall that the index should be tied to manufacturing sector wages. An index based on average manufacturing wages would be higher than an index based on all nonagricultural industries. If the index were based on service industries, which employ many low-wage workers, then there could be significant feedback on wages in this sector. An increase in the wage floor could boost service industry wages, which in turn would raise the minimum wage. This could once again increase service industry wages, only to repeat the cycle.

The minority of the House Committee on Education and Labor argued that indexing the minimum wage would be an inflationary move and would create one more source of automatic wage increases. Opponents also defended the legislative process on the ground that it allows lawmakers a degree of flexibility that would be lost in an automatic indexing system. During rounds of congressional hearings on FLSA, a lot more than just monetary compensation levels are reviewed. The process is also used to examine extending coverage, exemptions, compliance levels, overtime provisions, and other features of the FLSA. Since the FLSA is an important aspect of the federal government's labor market policy, congressional oversight is essential, and the periodic review can not be avoided if Congress is to discharge its responsibilities. The opponents glossed over the fact that indexation would not stop Congress from holding hearings, conducting investigations, and exercising oversight functions pertaining to the FLSA operations, including examinations of the index itself.

Beyond the concept of indexing, controversy over the specific percentage figures should not be ignored. The issue is not principles but pennies that add up to billions of dollars. Based on the past record of minimum wage increases, the Carter administration proposal—to set the index at 50 percent of hourly manufacturing wages—roughly equals the average peak of past increases. If the index were set at 47 percent of average manufacturing wages, then the minimum wage would be held at the relative level experienced during the 1950–77 period (Figure 15). Pegging the minimum wage at 53 percent was therefore a compromise among advocates favoring a higher level of relative minimum wage protection in comparison with the historical pattern. However, there is nothing magical about a 47-percent index, and it can be argued that in the welfare state, to encourage dependence upon work, a higher level of minimum wage protection than the historical average is in order.

Figure 15. The minimum wage has exceeded rises in the Consumer Price Index.

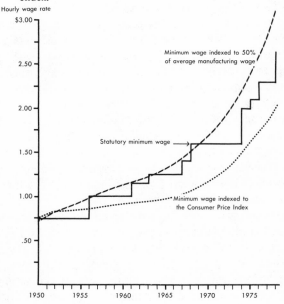

The Compromise Unravels

The delay during the summer recess was used by supporters to drum up more votes for the majority position. House floor debate on the FLSA amendments commenced in September, and the indexing formula, which was a central factor and a major innovation in the White House–labor compromise, was the first item on the agenda. Congressman John Erlenborn of Illinois proposed that starting in January 1978 the minimum wage be set at $2.65 an hour. The wage floor would then be increased to $2.85 in January 1979 and $3.05 at the start of 1980. These specific increases were to substitute for the index. In defense of his amendment, Erlenborn charged that adoption of indexation "will be signaling the policy of the United States to abandon the fight against inflation."[14] Backers of the Erlenborn amendment asserted that indexation would diminish congressional control over the wage floor.

Supporters of indexation argued that the proposed FLSA amendments would improve equity for low-wage workers, provide a higher degree of predictability than the ad hoc increases passed by Congress, and reduce the lags between inflationary spurts and a higher minimum wage.[15] Indexing the minimum wage would involve added costs, but there is no reason why we should be more dedicated and vigorous in fighting inflation when it affects the working poor than we are on behalf of other groups. Indeed, compassion for the lot of the working poor—the primary beneficiaries of minimum wage legislation—dictates that they should receive at least the same consideration as other groups whose needs may not be as pressing.

It would be absurd to blame the recent American experience with inflation on minimum wages, and backers of the Erlenborn amendment did not make such a charge. It was generally agreed that during most of the decade wages followed prices—the caboose at the end of the train was the minimum wage. Even an indexing formula based on a percentage of manufacturing wages would not change this order. Minimum wage workers would be able to regain losses due to inflation only after manufacturing workers won wage increases.

There is a good deal of truth to the economist's overworked axiom that there is no free lunch. A minimum wage index as formulated in the White House–labor compromise does not have the power to launch a new round of inflation, but it does institutionalize another form of cost-push inflation. A minimum wage index does involve a cost, and a wage floor index does make it slightly more difficult to wring out inflation from the system. Some critics charged that the White House–labor compromise on minimum wages could add more than one full percentage point to the annual rate of inflation. Although this seems to be on the very high end, suppose the wage floor changes would add only a fraction of a percentage point to inflation levels. On the theory that every little bit hurts, the minimum wage might be viewed in combination with other government regulations and actions. Individual government actions might not seem like much when viewed in isolation; but when the impacts of a textile quota, a steel tariff, a new environmental regulation, a higher minimum wage, and the entire range of government programs are added, the combined weight might have an appreciable impact on inflation. A few million here and some more elsewhere may add up to tidy sums that help fan inflation. If this is the case, then it becomes a question of whose interests will be sacrificed in the battle against inflation. Failure to adjust minimum wages because of inflationary concerns could place the poor in double jeopardy. Adding to their normal deprivation, failure to increase the minimum wage in line with price increases experienced in other sectors of society would also make the working poor bear the brunt of the burden caused by the shrinking value of the dollar.

The House adopted the Erlenborn amendment 223 to 193, and 97 Democrats joined an almost solid bloc of GOP representatives. This action killed the chances of an index being part of the 1977

FLSA amendments. Before the House floor action, the majority of the Senate Human Resources Committee had approved a bill that contained the major wage and indexing provisions of the White House–AFL-CIO compromise. However, after the House floor action organized labor and Senate allies conceded the indexing issue for 1977. Prior to Senate floor action, Senator Harrison A. Williams, Jr., of New Jersey, committee chairman, and Senator Jacob K. Javits of New York, the ranking Republican member on the committee, drafted an amendment to replace indexing. Under their amendment the minimum wage would increase in four steps: $2.65 in January 1978; $2.90 in January 1979; $3.15 in January 1980; and $3.40 in January 1981.

When the Senate considered the proposed minimum wage amendments in October 1977, opponents argued that the Williams-Javits amendment represented too large an increase. Senator John Tower of Texas charged that the proposed increase was in effect "back door indexing."[16] Instead, Tower proposed that the Senate adopt the minimum wage increase passed by the House. However, the Senate rejected this move (60 to 32) and then on a 76-to-14 vote adopted the Williams-Javits minimum wage proposals.

The final product to come out of the House-Senate conference tended to follow the more generous Senate bill. Similar to the Senate bill, an increase of four steps—instead of three—was adopted ($2.65 in January 1978; $2.90 in January 1979; $3.10 in January 1980; and $3.35 in January 1981). The third and fourth step increases were both 5 cents under the figures in the Senate bill. The House adopted the figures contained in the conference report (236 to 187) on October 20, 1977, and the Senate routinely approved the measure.

Wage Differentials

The early wage floors passed by the states did not contain one wage covering all workers. The FLSA during its initial years also provided for industry committees designed to establish different levels of protection for covered workers. A uniform wage does not provide the same degree of protection in all parts of the country. Differentials based on industry have been considered, as well as a subminimum wage for teenage workers. A system of FLSA wage differentials might produce some clear benefits. However, political, technical, and economic realities have proved effective obstacles to efforts at fine-tuning the wage floor.

Subminimum for Teenagers

During the 1977 round Congress fully considered wage differentials in the form of a subminimum wage for teenagers. Arguing that high minimum wages discouraged employers from hiring young and inexperienced workers, Representative Erlenborn proposed that a subminimum wage be established for workers under age 18, equal to 75 percent of the minimum wage for adults; workers between the ages of 18 and 21 would be paid the same subminimum wage during their first six months of employment. Representative Robert J. Cornell of Wisconsin proposed a more moderate differential that would have set the wage floor at 85 percent of the regular minimum for workers under 18 years of age during their first six months of employment. The stated goal of these amendments, as Cornell put it, was "to reduce the excessively high rate of unemployment among young people."[17]

Youth unemployment rates have been well over double—and more recently triple—the rate for adults during most of the postwar period. For black teen-agers and other minority youths the unemployment rate during the last business cycle rose to 40 percent, or more than five times the adult rate. Unemployment figures alone do not tell the full story, since they do not measure the quality of employment or the steadiness of a job. Inadequate work opportunities may also act as a real disincentive for many young workers to continue formal training or to pick up needed job skills.[18]

137

Indications are that the unemployment problems experienced during the teenage years linger on into adulthood. Basing their work on National Longitudinal Survey data, economists Arvil V. Adams and Garth L. Mangum found that unemployment leaves a lasting mark on teenagers; their average earnings are reduced, and they continue to have more than their share of work-related problems.[19] But how much, if any, of this youth unemployment can be blamed on the minimum wage? Cornell told his colleagues that he "would make no pretense that this piece of legislation will necessarily resolve the problem of youth unemployment. . . . Frankly, I do not know what effect this youth differential will have on youth unemployment or adult employment." But he hoped a lower minimum wage for younger workers would have the result "that more of our youth get off the streets and into productive employment."[20]

The 1977 round of FLSA amendments was not the first time a subminimum wage for young workers was considered by Congress. In 1971 the Nixon administration proposed the creation of a subminimum wage for teenagers. The AFL-CIO strongly opposed the proposal on the grounds that it would result in the displacement of adult workers, since the total number of jobs would not be increased. Also, organized labor argued that a lower wage for teenagers would diminish the work ethic among youths. It would also be discriminatory against teenagers, permitting employers who would be willing to pay the minimum wage to earn windfall profits.[21] Although the House committee rejected a subminimum wage in 1971, the full House adopted a proposal by Representative Erlenborn that would have established a differential rate for workers under 18 years of age and for full-time students under 21. The Erlenborn differential would have been 80 percent of the adult minimum, and it would have dropped the requirements for individual employer certifications. The Senate passed a bill that did not contain a youth subminimum, and the proposal died in conference. In 1973 Erlenborn and Representative John B. Anderson of Illinois revived the youth subminimum proposal. The idea was rejected on the House floor this time. One year later Congress passed minimum wage changes that were signed into law, but neither the Senate nor the House voted on the youth differential issue.

When the youth differential amendment was reintroduced in 1977, George Meany repeated the arguments used by organized labor against a youth subminimum in earlier years. A youth differential might work in the direction of evening out unemployment rates between different age groups, but this would not be a net benefit for society. "Does the Congress really want to say to teenagers," Meany questioned, "the only way to get you a job is to pay you less than the minimum wage and fire an older worker, who may have a family, so that you can be hired?"[22]

Existing Differentials

Although Congress rejected a universal differential based on age, it did recognize the rationale of wage differentials for inexperienced workers who learn on the job. Section 14 of the FLSA authorizes the Secretary of Labor to allow an employer to pay less than the minimum wage to full-time students, learners not in retail or service industries, and handicapped workers in sheltered workshops. Congress also has directed that no exemption be granted if there is a substantial possibility that adult employment would be hurt in the process.

In 1977 Congress examined these differentials for whatever guidance they might provide for a youth subminimum wage. The majority concluded that the exemptions took care of special cases and that no general wage differential was needed. The number of exemptions follows a pattern and reaches a peak after Congress passes an FLSA amendment (Figure 16). This number trends downward until the next general minimum wage increase. For the year ending June 1977 about 42,000 certificates were issued authorizing about 575,000 workers—three out of every four were

139

full-time students—to receive subminimum wages.[23] For full-time students the exemption is good as long as they remain in school. The duration for learner exemptions depends upon the occupation; the majority lasting several months. Handicapped workers must have the exemption renewed each year.

Figure 16. Exemptions from minimum wage protection have vastly increased since 1974.

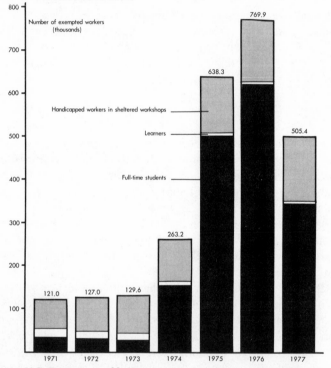

Source: U.S. Department of Labor.

During the 1977 congressional debate several lawmakers argued that the number of exemptions would be greater if there

140

were less bureaucratic red tape.[24] Overall the recipients of certificates were distributed as follows:

	Total exemptions (percent)
Restaurants and cafeterias	22
Variety department stores	20
Food stores	17
Motion picture theaters	17
Apparel and accessory stores	16
Universities and colleges	5
Agriculture	1
Other	2

It is difficult to use these data to predict what would happen if a general youth subminimum wage were introduced. While the Department of Labor keeps track of the number of certificates issued and the number of workers authorized to fill subminimum wage positions, it does not keep tabs on the number of jobs actually filled. Hence, the 1977 authorization of 575,000 exempt jobs does not mean that all of these positions were filled at the reduced minimum wage or even filled at all.

Since eating and drinking establishments have obtained the largest number of certificates, critics of a general subminimum wage have often called these proposals the fast-food industry amendments. In fact, the proposed youth differential amendment was frequently identified with McDonald's restaurants as representative of the fast-food industry.[25] However, other nationally known fast-food restaurants have gained even more exemption certificates than the producer of the Big Mac. Reflecting congressional interest in McDonald's, the Department of Labor reported to Congress on a utilization analysis of the food chain's full-time student certificates. McDonald's had received authority to employ students for 550,000 hours of work, but the company hired full-time students at less than the minimum wage for only 255,000 hours of work, utilizing only 46 percent of the subminimum wage authority.

141

The survey of McDonald's certificates demonstrates the problem of making quick calculations based on the number of certificates issued or positions authorized. The Labor Department has estimated that only about 60 percent of authorized student exemptions were used. Also, it is difficult to tell how many new jobs were created by the exemptions. A job given to, say, a full-time student at the expense of a nonstudent worker does not create a net job gain for society. There is no precise way of knowing how many employers pay the subminimum wage for positions that would have been filled at higher wages if no exemptions were granted. Given the nature of the data, the existing exemption program was used by both sides to "prove" their points in the youth subminimum wage debate.

Congressional Action

The opponents of the youth subminimum wage claimed that the demographic factors make this the wrong time to institute a youth wage differential. The boom period in teenage population growth is over, and the 1980s will witness a decline of about 8.5 percent in the teenage population.[26]

The projected decline in teenage population may have diminished, but it has not eliminated, the advocacy of a youth minimum wage differential. The transition from education—ended either by graduating or by dropping out—to steady or any employment can be a tortuous process for many youths who have few marketable skills. A lower youth wage, it is hoped, would ease this transition and also allow employers a period of time to increase the productivity of young workers so that in time their job performance would justify a higher wage. Typical of this line of reasoning was the testimony of the American Hotel and Motel Association's representative before Senate committee hearings. Three of every ten employees in the fast-food service industry are teenagers. A youth wage differential would make it profitable for fast-food establishments to employ more teenagers and provide them with the training and work experience leading to higher wages.[27] An executive of a restaurant chain told Congress: "Those who are unemployed because of inexperience and lack of skills need to have their productivity increased through job training opportunities."[28] The AFL-CIO's Lane Kirkland summed up the other side's response by insisting that a subminimum wage "has nothing to do with teenage unemployment. It is simply a device to give fast food operators and other employers a larger labor source to exploit."[29]

During the House floor debate Representative Parren Mitchell of Maryland insisted that the employment and training aspects of the subminimum wage were "a lot of malarkey. . . . A ghastly mistake. . . . Unemployment is chronic and deep across the board in the black community, and it does not make any sense at all to play one group of workers off against another."[30] Representatives Paul Simon, a cosponsor of the Cornell amendment, and Robert Michel, both from Illinois, noted that the institution of a subminimum wage was no longer a Republican party issue, as many Democratic lawmakers had shown sympathy for the need of a youth differential. Antidifferential representatives claimed that the impact of a lower wage floor for youths was not known and that American youths should not be made guinea pigs for testing economic theories.

The House rejected the Cornell amendment by 211 to 210. House Speaker Thomas P. O'Neill cast the deciding vote to beat down the proposal. Congressman Abner Mikva of Illinois saw the close vote as underscoring labor's problems on Capitol Hill: "Many members feel labor just doesn't represent many votes. They [organized labor] can't deliver votes any more, which always was much more important than the money they gave candidates."[31] The House vote also reflected a more effective lobbying effort on the part of business and industry trade groups.

The Senate Human Resources Committee rejected by a 10-to-4 vote an amendment by Senator Richard Schweiker of Pennsylvania that youths aged 16 to 19 be paid 75 percent of the minimum wage for the first six months of employment. Also, his amendment would have reduced the full-time student differential from 85 percent to 75 percent of the wage floor. However, the issue was taken to the Senate floor. The most radical proposed change came from Senator James A. McClure of Idaho in an amendment that would have exempted all teenagers from minimum wage protection. McClure's proposal went down to defeat 74 to 23. Senator Schweiker, after defeat in committee, introduced his 75-percent differential for workers under the age of 20 during the first six months of employment, insisting that his amendment would protect job opportunities for youths by establishing a special "entry-level" minimum wage for teenagers. "Aside from the evidence provided by academic research, common sense suggests that increases in the minimum wage adversely affect youth unemployment," he said. "Teenagers often have the least to offer in the labor market. They bring to the workplace disadvantages."[32] After voting down the 75-percent differential (55 to 38), the Senate also rejected a similar lower rate for workers aged 68 and over proposed by Senator William Scott of Virginia. Econometric research has concentrated on teenage labor markets and has almost ignored whatever impact minimum wages may have on older workers, whose productivity may decline with advanced age.

The Senate did adopt measures that give the Department of Labor more discretionary authority for the full-time student exemption program. Senator Dennis DeConcini of Arizona proposed increasing from four to six the number of full-time student exemptions a firm could employ without furnishing detailed records to the Department of Labor. The department was given added discretionary authority to remove the number limitation entirely if it found no evidence of adverse adult employment effects. This would seem to make it easier for firms to hire more full-time students at the differential rate, although before the 1977 amendments the department had granted numerous petitions for firms to hire more than 10 percent of their work force from this pool of workers.

Area Differentials

In addition to wage floor differentials based on age, Congress also dealt in the 1977 legislative round with regional differentials. But it ignored whatever economic justification may exist for the latter differentials and moved in the opposite direction. Puerto Rico and the Virgin Islands have a lower wage scale than the mainland, and minimum wage legislation reflected the differentials. A minimum wage that might have only minor employment effects in mainland labor markets could produce considerable injury in Puerto Rico. For this reason, the FLSA had established industry committees for these islands, which could set wage floors below the mainland level. By allowing wage differentials, it was hoped, the earnings of the working poor would be raised, while unemployment effects would be held to a minimum.

However, the 1977 amendments moved away from this system of wage differentials. Industry minimum wage rates already at the mainland minimum wage in Puerto Rico will remain the same as the mainland rates and will no longer be subject to industry committee review. Wage order rates that are less than the mainland minimum are to be automatically increased each January until the mainland rate is reached. Industry committees may review the wage order rates and increase them by amounts greater than those automatically required by the amendments. Wage orders that were between $2.00 and $2.30 an hour were increased by 25 cents an hour at the start of 1978. In January 1979 and at the start of each year thereafter, the hourly rate would be increased 30 cents until parity is reached. For wage orders that were under $2.00 per hour the 1978 increase was 25 cents an hour. The wage will be

145

increased by 25 cents an hour at the start of each year until $2.30 is reached, and after that the wage will be increased by 30 cents an hour until parity is reached.

The concept of wage differentials did not fare well in the 1977 round, and pressures to revive the issue in future reviews of minimum wage legislation may diminish in the 1980s. The South, which in the past has had the strongest claims for a regional differential, is rapidly catching up with other regions. The number of teen-agers is also going to decline in the 1980s, reducing pressures for a youth differential. Whatever benefits might have been derived from fine-tuning minimum wages, given the past difficulties and declining pressures, the outlook for minimum wage differentials is not promising.

Coverage

There is a clear relationship between FLSA coverage and the other policy decisions related to the minimum wage. If one goal is to minimize job losses, then the wage level set depends upon the degree of coverage. During the initial period of the FLSA many of the industries that employ the majority of teenagers were not covered. Under these conditions—and before the products of the postwar baby boom entered the labor market—the wage floor might have had only a marginal impact on youth labor markets. But as coverage was vastly expanded in the 1960s and 1970s, a greater number of traditional youth employers became subject to the wage floor. As a general rule, the broader the coverage of the wage floor, the lower the minimum wage should be if negative employment effects are to be minimized. Hence, the degree of coverage directly ties into the other minimum wage policy decisions.

In 1977 Congress reversed the movement of the preceding two decades toward expansion of coverage. The 1977 law removed an estimated 800,000 workers in small retail and service stores from FLSA coverage by raising the dollar volume exemption limits from $250,000 to $275,000 on July 1, 1978; to $325,000 on July

146

1, 1980; and to $362,500 on December 31, 1981. A related provision was the adoption of a measure to reduce the existing tip credit to 40 percent by 1981: an employer will be able to use only 40 percent of a worker's tips as a credit to lower the minimum paid to the employee.

Delay by Study Commission

Considering indexing, wage differentials, and coverage, Congress in 1977 grappled with several basic FLSA issues that could potentially have overhauled the system. But Congress decided to move cautiously. The majority was apparently persuaded by Representative Carl Perkins of Kentucky, chairman of the House Education and Labor Committee, that Congress was being asked to vote on issues "that simply have not been addressed in depth by congressional study commission or by any totally independent study commission since the inception of the law on minimum wage standards."[33] The House adopted, by a vote of 301 to 118, an amendment creating the Minimum Wage Study Commission, and the final bill passed by Congress sided with the House on this matter.

As part of the final law, two commission members each were appointed by the secretaries of Labor, Commerce, Agriculture, and Health, Education, and Welfare.[34] The commission was mandated to report by 1981 on the gamut of issues relating to the FLSA. Specifically the commission is mandated to cover the following areas:

1. The overall effectiveness of the wage floor in ameliorating destitution

2. The degree of inflationary impact, if any, caused by the FLSA

3. The ripple effect on the minimum wage; i.e., the impact of the wage floor on wages paid to employees whose earnings are higher than the legislative minimum

4. The economic consequences of an automatic index

147

5. The employment or unemployment effects on young, handicapped, and aged workers

6. The full-time student certification program and other exemptions

7. The overall level of noncompliance with the FLSA and

8. The demographic profile of minimum wage workers.

In addition to the report, due in three years, Congress also mandated that the commission report back in one year on the extent of FLSA exemptions granted to conglomerate corporations. The concern is that a subsidiary of a company with sales volume in the millions of dollars might be granted FLSA exemptions under the small business provisions of the act. The commission also has been charged to report back on the economic consequences of eliminating this exemption for larger conglomerates.

Aside from the hope of gaining fresh insights into the economic consequences of minimum wage legislation, the creation of a new commission was also used by both sides of the minimum wage debate as an argument for delaying any radical changes in the FLSA. Anti-indexing forces used the creation of the commission as a reason for holding off on any action in this area, while lawmakers against a subminimum wage for teenagers employed similar logic for delaying action on that front.

The 1977 round of FLSA amendments in a very real sense was a holding operation, and several crucial policy issues were not resolved. Yet hope springs eternal, and the creation of a new commission indicates that policymakers desire more hard evidence in making basic decisions. Whether social scientists can deliver the data needed by the policymakers remains to be seen.

6

Minimum Wages in the Welfare State

"Work keeps at bay three great evils: boredom, vice and need," Voltaire wrote.[1] Whatever appeal this observation may have had two centuries ago, it falls short of universal acceptance in today's economy. Although work provides self-fulfillment for some individuals, many jobs still require constant repetition of menial and monotonous tasks. It is doubtful whether such jobs eliminate boredom, considering that the rewards for work in many cases do not free workers from Voltaire's third evil, want.

Just because an individual is employed, even in a full-time job, it does not necessarily mean that the person or the worker's family is receiving an income above the poverty threshold. Millions of family heads are active workers but still cannot support their families at a minimally acceptable level above the formally recognized destitution index. Despite improvements, about 12 percent of the United States population still remains in poverty. Federal, state, and local efforts are directed to get unemployed persons or some who are outside of the labor force—including public assistance recipients—into productive employment. But if the wages paid are excessively low, then work will not keep poverty at bay.

More than two out of three adults in the poverty pool of potential workers did work during the year. In 1977 more than 5 million workers were in the labor force for 40 weeks or more, earned less than an annualized minimum wage, and also were members of families that had a total income of less than 150 percent of the poverty level. For whites this represented almost 6 percent of those with 40 weeks' or more attachment to the labor force; for blacks and for female-headed families it was over 15 percent.

The needs of those who are already laboring at low-paying jobs have often been lost sight of in training and job creation efforts, although millions of Americans cannot work their way out of poverty. Given the economic conditions of low-wage labor markets, this situation is not likely to change in the near future. To date, the minimum wage has been the most direct and comprehensive policy tool for improving the lot of the working poor.

What Have We Learned?

Few government policies have been run through more statistical and econometric tests than the minimum wage. But quantity is not to be confused with quality. The methodology used in many wage floor studies appears to be flawed, and their conclusions are highly suspect. However, with recent developments in data collection, methodology, and computer technology, a growing number of researchers have attempted to conduct more sophisticated statistical minimum wage tests. Yet, even with these advances, hard-and-fast quantitative results have remained elusive. Respectable studies have come down on all sides of the issues. Inquiries that have agreed on the basic direction of minimum wage impacts have differed about the magnitude of these results. That the minimum wage creates some unemployment does not help policymakers in drafting a wage floor program. More important is *how much* unemployment is created by the wage floor.

The conclusions advanced by researchers depend upon the assumptions they make as well as on the variables, data, and equations they use. These basic decisions must be made by the researcher and cannot be left to a computer. The data selected and the models constructed in effect contain the researcher's basic assumptions as to how our economy functions. Since no one economic paradigm is held by all researchers, it is a natural result that numerous and different basic models will be applied to minimum wage investigations. Vast differences in quantitative findings hinge upon the different assumptions and structures that have been employed. The analyses, admittedly reflecting the normative judgments of the authors, suggest the following conclusions:

1. The dire predictions made by neoclassical economic theorists concerning the impact of minimum wages on aggregate unemployment attest to their biases and are not supported by empirical research. The best evidence suggests that the minimum wage has *not* been a major cause of unemployment. Some job loss due to the wage floor has been detected, but it is much smaller than claimed by orthodox economists.

2. However, what is true for the whole economy might not be true for all of its parts. Selected labor markets may be more sensitive to minimum wages than others. Teenage labor markets, for example, do not appear to be immune from negative impacts caused by minimum wages. But this is not the same as saying that minimum wages are the primary cause of youth unemployment. Econometric evidence indicates that even without any minimum wage, the post–World War II period still would have seen high rates of youth unemployment. General business conditions, demographic forces, population migration, the influx of undocumented aliens, the extension of the welfare state, and changing societal attitudes—including more women in the work force and longer education—all appear to influence youth labor markets far more than minimum wages. Added to these primary factors, the minimum wage does ·seem to involve some costs in the form

151

of reducing youth employment levels. Also, the minimum wage may be responsible in part for increasing the number of young workers who wind up with part-time jobs instead of full-time employment. There is no free lunch. Yet minimum wages cannot explain the full extent of youth unemployment—or even a majority of it. Also, econometric estimates have not been able to agree on the size of these social costs.

3. A favorite model used to "prove" the damaging impact of minimum wages is one that ignores demographic factors. In the language of economists, these researchers consider only the demand for labor but not changes in the supply. Analysts who have considered the latter factor have often found that wage floor results lose any real significance. In some cases the researchers bent on proving negative minimum wage impacts ignore the demands of the military for youth and the impact of training and employment efforts.

4. The statistical conclusions about the wage floor also depend upon the interaction of supply and demand forces. The assumption that the economy shows a good deal of wage and price flexibility leads to the conclusion that minimum wages appear to have a strong negative impact on labor markets. However, if the American economy demonstrates a propensity for wage and price rigidities, then conclusions about the harmful impact of minimum wages are vastly reduced. The latter assumption concerning wage and price rigidities provides a much more realistic picture of the American economy.

5. The varying conclusions reached by different researchers often depend upon which limited aspect of the wage floor issue a researcher considers. The vast majority of minimum wage studies have been concerned with the employment and unemployment effects of the wage floor. Just because the minimum wage involves job losses, it does not necessarily damn the statutory wage rate. These social costs in most cases appear to be more than compensated for the by the social benefits produced by the minimum wage.

The few studies that have ventured beyond the confines of employment and unemployment have found other results caused by the minimum wage. For example, studies have shown that employers often respond to the minimum wage by efforts to raise productivity, improve training, and change work schedules. Despite indications that these variables have a dramatic impact on the results caused by the wage floor, few studies have tried to investigate these ramifications.

6. A controlling factor that has moderated the positive as well as the negative impacts of the minimum wage has been the restraint exercised by Congress in determining the level of the minimum wage. If the minimum wage were vastly boosted to, say, 75 percent of the average wage in the manufacturing sector, then some of the dire predictions might come true. Just because unemployment effects have been modest with the minimum wage pegged to about 50 percent of the average wage, it does not mean it would be either safe or wise to set minimum wages at a much higher and untested relative level.

7. Since minimum wages involve a tradeoff of higher wages for a slightly diminished opportunity to find work, one must also consider the income side of the minimum wage equation. It has only been in recent years that researchers have tried to deal with these income-related impacts. The statistical evidence indicates that the wage floor has the power to increase significantly the wages paid to the working poor. Minimum wages may produce some unemployment and other negative results for adult workers, but the income gains due to the wage floor are far greater than any injury.

On balance adult workers appear to be made better off under the wage floor. For teenagers the tradeoff is more pronounced. Although the gains from minimum wages are clear, the opportunities to find full-time employment are reduced for young workers. However, recent studies indicate that even for young workers the income gains are greater than the negative side effects.

153

8. It should not come as a surprise that the minimum wage does not vastly alter the pattern of income distribution within the American economy. Indeed, minimum wage legislation was never intended as a primary policy tool for achieving this goal. Minimum wages might not be the perfectly efficient policy tool in fighting destitution; nevertheless the wage floor does appear to have a statistically significant impact in reducing destitution within American society.

Alternative Tools

In the past too many analysts who damned the minimum wage did not suggest policy alternatives to help the working poor. The best they could offer was the old advice, Let them eat cake. This situation has changed as a growing number of researchers have suggested options to minimum wages as a means of dealing with low-wage problems. A few have argued that the wage mechanism might not be the best tool for meeting minimal family income needs. If free market forces result in income levels below some societal minimum, then the government could make up the difference.

According to this view a guaranteed income for working heads of households may have advantages over a minimum wage that would provide the same income. An unskilled and occasionally unemployed sole supporter of a family needs a higher minimum wage than does a youth working after school or a second family wage earner working part time. A guaranteed income could be more selective than the minimum wage, helping those who have the most serious needs without raising standards for all workers and the labor costs for all employers. Reliance on the wage mechanism alone precludes raising out of poverty workers with numerous dependents. Boosting everyone's wage to the level required in the above case might have dire consequences to many intended beneficiaries of the legislation.

However, a guaranteed income is likely to have other undesirable effects on labor market behavior. Policymakers have thus far failed to design a formula that would guarantee a basic income level without acting as a disincentive to work. Yet, even if this difficult problem can be resolved, a guaranteed income would not make the minimum wage superfluous. There is much to be said for encouraging people to depend upon earnings rather than upon income support. The difficulty is to design a system that pays more for working than for not working, and a strong and effective minimum wage aids in this design effort. Also, workers should be protected from exploitation. In the real world, which is far different from economic models based upon perfect competition, some form of minimum wage regulation is required even from the point of view of allocative efficiency—not to mention equity. Equally important is the need to encourage workers to become economically independent and to rise above the poverty threshold without relying upon income supplements. A guaranteed income without a minimum wage may also drive down the earnings of workers; rather than aiding the working poor, the guarantee could be subverted into a windfall to employers at the expense of the federal budget deficit. The minimum wage is, therefore, needed as a floor to express the socially recognized value of labor rather than just to meet income needs.

American society appears still to place a high value on the work ethic. In considerations of possible welfare reform, the minimum wage has an important role to play in healthy maintenance of the work ethic. Without a wage floor that is kept in line with changing price levels and growth in productivity, the income gained from welfare could outpace the rewards obtained from work for millions of Americans. Welfare could then become an increasingly rational alternative to work for a growing number of individuals and families. The choice between work and welfare is not an easy decision, as the widespread incidence of supplementing earnings from work with welfare already suggests. Almost three out of five

155

families receiving Aid to Families with Dependent Children also have some labor market earnings. A breadwinner with three dependents in a state that pays high welfare benefits, such as Michigan or New York, would need a full-time job paying in excess of $4.00 per hour (in 1978 dollars) to match the value of maximum combined cash support, food stamp grants, and other in-kind assistance for a four-member family.

For these reasons, the minimum wage is tied up with the issue of welfare reform. A change in the income support system without a strong wage floor can tip the scales against work and result in higher welfare program costs. This is one way in which quick assessments of the minimum wage often fail to consider all the possible forces at work. For example, increasing the minimum wage might have some inflationary impact on prices. But if the minimum wage were not increased, the relative rewards from work would diminish, making welfare an attractive alternative. Not increasing the minimum wage could result in higher welfare costs and a larger budget deficit to finance the programs. To the degree that federal budget deficits contribute to inflation, then *not* increasing the minimum wage might also have an inflationary impact on the economy. Hence, the impact of the minimum wage cannot be considered in isolation from other social policies and economic forces. Minimum wages have a role in the policy mix of income support programs. Research and policy proposals that fail to interconnect minimum wages and other income alternatives, including the massive system of transfer payments, are not dealing with a major part of the total picture.

The minimum wage has played an important role in welfare reform proposals during the 1970s, although this role has not always been enunciated. The Carter administration's goal was to stimulate welfare recipients' work efforts through massive public job creation efforts. While the words "income guarantee" were not used, under the Carter proposal all destitute Americans would be eligible to receive a basic level of federal cash aid. Beyond this, those who can and do work would wind up receiving more income at jobs paying the minimum wage. Even with the FLSA 1977 amendments, this work incentive may not have been particularly attractive; but without the 1977 increases it would have been almost nonexistent. Without a vigorous minimum wage policy, reformation of our income support system could fail to bring about the desired results.

Minimum wages started as a modest effort to protect some of the working poor from exploitation in labor markets. In the welfare state the role of the minimum wage has been expanded to protect overall societal values by striving to make work a more lucrative alternative than dependence. The current income support system does little for the working poor, and the minimum wage has been the prime program designed for this portion of the population. However, the minimum wage is not the only tool that could help destitute workers. Congress has already tried other methods to complement the minimum wage, including an earned income tax credit and a new jobs tax credit.

Neither program makes the minimum wage superfluous. The employee tax credit increases the net rewards from work efforts; the employer tax credit is designed to reduce in part the cost of added labor to the firm. A more direct method to help the working poor and increase employment has been wage subsidy proposals. Yet, interestingly enough, most wage rate subsidy proposals do not obviate the need for a vigorous minimum wage program. In fact, more often than not the wage floor system is given an explicit role in wage subsidy proposals.

In general, wage rate subsidies reduce the labor costs of an employer. Most wage subsidy proposals would require the government to supplement the wages paid to designated workers. The hourly payment could be equal to some percentage of the difference between a target wage and a worker's actual wage. With the government picking up the wage subsidy bill, the income obtained from work would not be diminished, and there would not be a negative impact on the incentive to work. At the same time the net effect would be to make labor a cheaper resource for employers, and it is argued that the wage subsidies would induce firms to hire more workers and use more labor-intensive production methods. Instead of using the government to regulate wages, the market forces of supply and demand would set wage rates, and the government would pick up the tab to bring all earnings to a predetermined, socially agreed target level.[2]

It is charged that one fault of minimum wage programs is that many low-wage workers are not members of destitute families. But a wage rate subsidy system also could suffer from problems of targeting protection to the needy only. Econometric simulations have shown that a universal wage subsidy system would experience targeting problems similar to those of the minimum wage.[3] Some wage rate subsidy plans propose a system in which voucher cards would be issued to eligible workers, who would hand them over to employers. Workers would then be paid additional wages equal to the difference between their nominal hourly wage and a target wage. The voucher cards would be handed back to the government with the required forms, and the government would pay the employer the subsidy.

But a wage rate subsidy program would not obviate the need for a minimum wage. In fact, many proposals peg the subsidy to the minimum wage, although the number of children in a family and the cost of living may also be considered in determining the size of the subsidy. For example, a family head with two children might have a target wage equal to 130 percent of the minimum wage, while a family head with three children would have a target wage equal to, say, 150 percent of the minimum wage.

Advocates of wage subsidy plans argue that the cost to the federal government per job created would be less under wage subsidy programs than under traditional job creation methods. Some computer simulations predict that wage subsidy programs can have a dramatic impact on increasing employment levels.[4] However, wage subsidy programs are not without their potential problems and abuses. The goal of wage subsidy programs is not to provide windfall profits to employers; rather, the hope is to reach different social goals. Small-scale efforts to induce private sector employment for the disadvantaged have been largely unsuccessful so far. Very little is known about the use of government subsidies for private employers, as verified by the poor records of employers taking advantage of tax credits for hiring and employing public assistance recipients and applying for reimbursement to cover extra costs involved in hiring and retaining deficiently prepared workers from poor households.

The selection of employers qualifying to receive subsidies remains a major problem. The goal is not to subsidize the private sector to offer the same jobs or hire the same workers that they would in the absence of a subsidy. There is also the problem that employer knowledge of the subsidy could lead some firms to reduce wages at the government's expense. A wage subsidy system might favor expanding firms as well as growing regions. Benefits would go mainly to rapidly expanding firms and areas that need help the least, and the subsidy could result in windfalls for new hires that would have occurred without the subsidies.

Although wage subsidy programs and welfare reform proposals might be far from a godsend, they all share an interesting common feature—the role of the minimum wage would be enhanced, not diminished. In the fight against destitution, the minimum wage would be given added functions. For this reason the minimum wage system takes on even greater importance than it had during its first four decades.

The alternative policy tool of a youth subminimum wage has also been suggested. Conceptually, a lower youth wage might be a desirable policy, but the 1980s would be the wrong time to institute it. Beyond the evidence that the minimum wage has not been the prime factor causing youth employment problems, demographic forces argue against such a change. Because of decreased birth rates in the 1960s and 1970s, the bulge of teenagers entering the labor force has passed, and the growth in the supply of young workers will be diminishing in the future. Subsidies to the private sector as a way of employing more young workers have not shown a very impressive track record in the past. There are many real structural and cultural factors causing high youth unemployment rates. Facing up to these difficult issues—instead of taking the easy escape of pointing at the minimum wage—will provide real solutions in this problem area. There is some truth to the old saying, You get what you pay for. It is impossible to make work an attractive alternative for young workers if their earnings are allowed to fall through the cracks of a modest wage floor. The FLSA already allows employers to pay full-time students, learners, and certain handicapped workers a subminimum wage. The exemptions are not difficult to obtain in general, but teenagers often refuse to work at a subminimum wage.

For related reasons the concept of indexing the minimum wage makes a good deal of sense. Inflation and wage gains in other sectors erode the protection passed by Congress. Since Congress has shown a pattern of passing a minimum wage of roughly 50 percent of the average in the manufacturing sector, an index could make this level of FLSA protection a continuing reality. An index of this magnitude would provide a degree of minimum wage stability in place of the current periodic legislative rounds with their uncertain results. If the index were set too high, then some of the negative consequences predicted by traditional economic theory might materialize. But a modest index seems in order and would not hinder congressional oversight of the FLSA program.

The Bottom Line

In the absence of an econometric breakthrough, it appears that we will continue to know a lot less about the actual results of minimum wages than we would like. The possible margin of error remains significant. In the end we are left with educated guesses that are nothing more than first approximations. Congress has recognized that it is being called on to legislate difficult problems without an adequate factual footing and has mandated the establishment of the Minimum Wage Study Commission. While this decision is to be welcomed, the caveats of the commission members should be heeded. As one commissioner put it, "I do not visualize a world in which a study is completed that . . . will be generally acceptable. . . . So even if we do the very best series of studies be prepared for criticism."[5] Wage floor analysis remains in part an art that cannot be totally divorced from value judgments.

Even given these uncertainties, our conclusion is that the minimum wage has served a highly useful function. Policy assessment is built on normative as much as on technical foundations, and notions of success or failure are relative. The negative spillovers caused by the minimum wage are too frequently overstated. No matter how desirable a change, it is likely to have some undesirable side effects. Even in the case of teenagers the social costs do not appear to be unmanageable, although the costs are considerable. Based on a range of studies, it appears that a 25-percent increase in the minimum wage would reduce youth employment by between 3.5 and 5.5 percent. Any wage losses due to unemployment must be balanced by the benefits, or income gains, due to higher wages received by workers who retain jobs. Given these estimates of an inelastic demand for young workers, the income gains appear to be larger than the social costs.

Concerning inflation, any wage increase in excess of improved productivity contributes to a higher price level. Raising the wage floor can add to inflationary pressures. However, aside from unreconstructed neoclassical economic ideology, there is little evidence that low-wage workers are being paid according to the value of their marginal product. Increasing the minimum wage is not inflationary if it prevents undue advantages to employers and forces more efficient and equitable use of labor. Another goal of the wage floor is to use the government to protect the interests of low-wage workers in an economy where other groups are pressing for wage or profit gains by exercising market power. In this case, the inflationary consequences of the minimum wage may be justified as compensatory, and the wage gains that need to be checked are those won by vested interests with market power.

In essence, then, reluctance to utilize the minimum wage to maintain the well-being of low-wage workers, much less to improve their relative position, is not based on documentation of massive unemployment or inflationary pressures. Rather, it appears to be founded on the belief that any job is better than no job, that the availability of employment is much more important than the quality of the job, and that labor markets are perfectly competitive and just in allocating wages and employment opportunities according to economic theories based on marginal productivity concepts. All of these are arguable assumptions. The belief that work will eliminate poverty is an incorrect assumption for millions of families. There is no proof that the minimum wage causes massive problems, and there is a great deal of evidence supporting its positive contributions to society.

Institutional Changes

The American economy has undergone vast institutional and economic changes since the FLSA was passed in 1938. When society experiences dramatic shifts, it is necessary to reexamine whether old policies still make sense under new conditions. The minimum wage is an appropriate illustration.

The federal experience with placing a floor under wages started during the depths of the Great Depression. The goal was to eliminate excessively low wages and to raise the earnings of the working poor. Despite institutional changes and a vast improvement in our nation's standard of living, the problems of low-wage labor markets remain. The reality of work and poverty is still true for millions of Americans, albeit that the standard has been raised. Exploitation may not be a fashionable word, but the ability to take advantage of those on the lower rungs of society and the labor force still must be faced. For these reasons the wage floor makes just as much sense now as when it was first created.

Indeed, other developments make the minimum wage even more important now than when the FLSA was formed. In 1938 the wage floor's primary role was to protect unorganized workers who lacked the market power to protect their own interests. The New Deal might have set the social policy ball rolling, but the role of the public sector was still far less than it is in today's mature welfare state. Whether we condemn or praise it, the welfare state is a fact of life and is not about to wither away. Social welfare efforts are not a mere appendage to the economy, for they have become an integral part of the system and have altered society in many fundamental ways. They affect the way we do business, and they certainly have had a major impact on labor markets. Under these conditions a wage floor is required to do much more than just police labor market conditions in the private sector.

Clearly our society must avoid paying individuals on welfare more than they can earn for working. The economic and social consequences of ignoring this obvious maxim would be disastrous. Yet we can not have our cake and eat it too.

A compassionate and affluent society that moves beyond the limited bounds of strict laissez-faire must also ensure that work pays more than subsistence or welfare. The minimum wage now has an added social function that was not even considered when the FLSA was drafted in the late 1930s. The maintenance of a vigorous work ethic, in the realm of the welfare state, will become increasingly difficult without a strong wage floor.

Evaluations of the minimum wage experience frequently suffer because its impact is compared with some ideal system or because only one limited aspect of the wage floor is explored. On the basis of these faulty research standards, the minimum wage program is often judged to be a failure. However, this is a misleading ground for comparison. A meaningful evaluation of the wage floor must consider and weigh the realistic economic, social, and political alternatives. Even though the minimum wage may directly affect only a limited number of workers, the larger picture shows that the wage floor is a pervasive force affecting diverse segments of society. The minimum wage will continue to have an increasing impact on the type of society we envisage and in fact create.

Notes

Chapter 1

1. U.S. Department of Labor, Employment Standards Administration, *Minimum Wage and Maximum Hours Standards under the Fair Labor Standards Act* (Washington: Government Printing Office, 1978), pp. 45–46.

2. Ibid., p. 61.

3. See, for example, two editorials: "The Cruel Cost of the Minimum Wage," *New York Times,* August 17, 1977; and "The Wages of Trade," *New York Times,* June 5, 1977.

4. Chase Manhattan Bank, *Business in Brief,* June 1966, p. 3.

5. Robert S. Goldfarb, "The Policy Content of Quantitative Minimum Wage Research," *Annual Proceedings of the Industrial Relations Research Association* (Madison, Wis.: Industrial Relations Research Association, 1974), p. 261.

6. U.S. Congress, Senate Committee on Human Resources, Subcommittee on Labor, *Hearings on the 1977 Amendments to the Fair Labor Standards Act* ·(Washington: Government Printing Office, 1977), p. 179.

7. U.S. Department of Commerce, Bureau of the Census, *Money Income and Poverty Status of Families and Persons in the United States: 1976* (Washington: Government Printing Office, September 1977), series P-60, no. 107, p. 29.

8. U.S. Congressional Budget Office, *Poverty Status of Families under Alternative Definitions of Income* (Washington: Government Printing Office, October 1977), Paper No. 17, p. 29; and U.S. Department of Health, Education, and Welfare, *The Measure of Poverty* (Washington: Government Printing Office, April 1976), pp. 7–11, 19–20.

9. U.S. Department of Commerce, op. cit., pp. 17, 25.

10. Unpublished tabulations derived from Current Population Survey, March 1978.

11. U.S. Department of Labor, Employment Standards Administration, *Estimated Cumulative Percentage Distribution of Nonsupervisory Farm Workers*

Subject to the Minimum Wage Provision of FLSA by Average Straight-Time Hourly Earnings, U.S., December 31, 1976, p. 1.

12. Charles T. Stewart, Jr., *Low Wage Workers in an Affluent Society* (Chicago: Nelson-Hall Co., 1974), pp. 16–17; George E. Delehanty and Robert Evans, Jr., "Low-Wage Employment: An Inventory and an Assessment" (Cambridge, Mass.: M.I.T. Press, 1969); Vera C. Perrella, "Low Earners and Their Incomes," *Monthly Labor Review,* May 1967, pp. 35–40; and Steven Sternlieb and Alvin Bauman, "Employment Characteristics of Low-Wage Workers," *Monthly Labor Review,* July 1965, pp. 11–12.

13. Stewart, op. cit., pp. 16–17.

14. Glen G. Cain, "The Challenge of Segmented Labor Market Theories to Orthodox Theory: A Survey," *Journal of Economic Literature,* December 9, 1976, pp. 1215–57.

15. Victor R. Fuchs, *The Service Economy* (New York: National Bureau of Economic Research, 1968), pp. 22–24.

16. Harold Wool, *The Labor Supply for Lower Level Occupations,* U.S. Department of Labor Monograph 42 (Washington: Government Printing Office, 1976), pp. 100–103.

17. Ibid., pp. 72–73.

Chapter 2

1. N. Arnold Tolles, "American Minimum Wage Laws: Their Purposes and Results," *Annual Proceedings of the Industrial Relations Research Association* (Madison, Wis.: Industrial Relations Research Association, 1959), pp. 116–17.

2. Henry Pelling, *American Labor* (Chicago: University of Chicago Press, 1960), pp. 4–6, 228.

3. Harry A. Millis and Royal E. Montgomery, *The Economics of Labor* (New York: McGraw-Hill Book Company, 1938), 1, 305–6.

4. Elizabeth Brandeis, "Labor Legislation," in John R. Commons et al., *History of Labor in the United States* (New York: Macmillan Company, 1935), p. 511.

5. As quoted in John R. Commons and John B. Andrews, *Principles of Labor Legislation* (New York: Augustus M. Kelley, 1967), p.. 44.

6. Ibid., pp. 46–47; and Brandeis, op. cit., p. 536.

7. Alfred Marshall, *Principles of Economics* (London: Macmillan Press, 1920), p. 595.

8. Philip Taft, *Economics and Problems of Labor* (Harrisburg, Pa.: Stackpole Company, 1955), p. 240.

9. Glenn W. Miller, *American Labor and the Government* (New York: Prentice-Hall, 1948), p. 149.

10. Millis and Montgomery, op. cit., pp. 307–10.

11. U.S. Department of Commerce, Bureau of the Census, *Historical Statistics of the United States* (Washington: Government Printing Office, 1957), pp. 125–27.

12. Walter Lippmann, "The Campaign against Sweating," *New Republic,* March 27, 1915, p. 8.

13. Arthur M. Schlesinger, Jr., *The Age of Roosevelt: The Politics of Upheaval* (Boston: Houghton Mifflin Co., 1960), p. 479.

14. As quoted in Ronald A. Anderson, *Government and Business* (Cincinnati, Ohio: South-Western Publishing Co., 1966), pp. 36–37.

15. As quoted in Miller, op. cit., p. 229.

16. Schlesinger, op. cit., p. 271.

17. R. W. Fleming, "The Significance of the Wagner Act," in Milton Derber and Edwin Young, eds., *Labor and the New Deal* (Madison, Wis.: University of Wisconsin Press, 1957), p. 126.

18. Broadus Mitchell, *Depression Decade: From New Era through New Deal, 1929-1941* (New York: Holt Rinehard and Winston, 1962), pp. 242–44, 284.

19. Murray Edelman, "New Deal Sensitivity to Labor Interests," in Derber and Young, op. cit., p. 170.

20. Anderson, op. cit., p. 41.

21. John W. Chambers, "The Big Switch: Justice Roberts and the Minimum Wage Cases," *Labor History,* Winter 1969, p. 44.

22. Pelling, op. cit., p. 163; and Jonathan Grossman, "Fair Labor Standards Act of 1938: Maximum Struggle for a Minimum Wage," *Monthly Labor Review*, June 1978, pp. 25–26.

23. Grossman, op. cit., p. 29.

24. Robert S. Goldfarb, "An Analysis of Minimum Wages," unpublished, pp. 10–11.

25. U.S. Department of Labor, Division of State Employment Standards, "Minimum Wage Rates Applicable to Nonsupervisory Nonfarm Employment," February 1, 1978 (processed).

26. U.S. Department of Labor, Employment Standards Administration, *Minimum Wage and Maximum Hours Standards under the Fair Labor Standards Act* (Washington: Government Printing Office, 1978), pp. 21–22.

27. Edward M. Gramlich, "Impact of Minimum Wages on Other Wages, Employment, and Family Incomes," *Brookings Papers on Economic Activity,* 2:1976, pp. 422–24.

28. Orley Ashenfelter and Robert Smith, *Compliance with the Minimum Wage Law,* Technical Analysis Paper 19A, rev. (Washington: U.S. Department of Labor, 1977), pp. 3–16.

Chapter 3

1. Paul A. Samuelson, *Economics* (New York: McGraw-Hill Book Company, 1973), p. 1.

2. George J. Stigler, "The Economist and the State,"*American Economic Review,* March 1965, pp. 16–17.

3. George J. Stigler, "The Economics of Minimum-Wage Legislation," *American Economic Review,* June 1946, pp. 359–60.

4. Richard Lester, "Marginalism, Minimum Wages, and Labor Markets," *American Economic Review,* March 1947, pp. 142–45.

5. Marie L. Obenauer and Bertha Von Der Nienburg, *The Effect of Minimum Wage Determinations in Oregon,* Women's Bureau Bulletin 176 (Washington: U.S. Department of Labor, 1915).

6. Allan M. Cartter and F. Ray Marshall, *Labor Economics: Wages, Employment, and Trade Unionism* (Homewood, Ill.: Richard D. Irwin, 1972), p. 342.

7. U.S. Department of Labor, Wage and Hour Division, "Minimum Wages in the Seamless Hosiery Industry," 1941 (processed).

8. A. F. Hinrichs, "Effects of the 25-Cent Minimum Wage on Employment in the Seamless Hosiery Industry," *Journal of the American Statistical Association,* March 1940, pp. 18–19.

9. U.S. Department of Labor, Bureau of Labor Statistics, "Wages in the Pants, Shirts, and Allied Garment Industries," 1941 (processed).

10. U.S. Department of Labor, *Results of the Minimum-Wage Increase of 1950* (Washington: Government Printing Office, 1954).

11. U.S. Department of Labor, *Studies of the Economic Effects of the $1.00 Minimum Wage* (Washington: Government Printing Office, 1957), pp. 3–6.

12. Louis E. Badenhoop, "Effects of the $1 Minimum Wage in Seven Areas," *Monthly Labor Review,* July 1958, pp. 737–43.

13. John M. Peterson and Charles T. Stewart, Jr., *Employment Effects of Minimum Wage Rates* (Washington: American Enterprise Institute, 1969), p. 113.

14. U.S. Department of Labor, *An Evaluation of the Minimum Wage and Maximum Hours Standards of the Fair Labor Standards Act* (Washington: Government Printing Office, January 1965), pp. 13–17.

15. U.S. Department of Labor, Employment Standards Administration, *Minimum Wage and Maximum Hours Standards under the Fair Labor Standards Act* (Washington: Government Printing Office, 1968), p. 1.

16. U.S. Department of Labor, Employment Standards Administration, *Minimum Wage and Maximum Hours Standards under the Fair Labor Standards Act* (Washington: Government Printing Office, 1970), pp. 2–3.

17. U.S. Department of Labor, Employment Standards Administration, *Minimum Wage and Maximum Hours Standards under the Fair Labor Standards Act* (Washington: Government Printing Office, 1969), pp. 12–13.

18. U.S. Department of Labor, Employment Standards Administration, *Minimum Wage and Maximum Hours Standards under the Fair Labor Standards Act* (Washington: Government Printing Office, 1971), pp. 2–3.

19. U.S. Department of Labor, Employment Standards Administration, *Minimum Wage and Maximum Hours Standards under the Fair Labor Standards Act* (Washington: Government Printing Office, 1972), p. 8.

20. U.S. Department of Labor, *Hired Farm Workers* (Washington: Government Printing Office, 1972), pp. 21–24.

21. AFL-CIO, *Special Report: Minimum Wages* (Washington: AFL-CIO, 1977), p. 2; and Clarence Mitchell, "Outworn Myths Means Present Misery: The Minimum Wage Should Provide a Living," *Viewpoint,* 3:1977, pp. 20–21.

Chapter 4

1. Thomas Gale Moore, "The Effects of Minimum Wages on Teenage Unemployment Rates," *Journal of Political Economy,* July-August 1971, pp. 897–902.

2. Douglas K. Adie, "Teenage Unemployment and Real Federal Minimum Wages," *Journal of Political Economy,* March-April 1973, pp. 435–41; and Douglas K. Adie, "The Lag in the Effect of Minimum Wages on Teenage Unemployment," *Annual Proceedings of the Industrial Relations Research Association* (Madison, Wis.: Industrial Relations Research Association, 1971), pp. 38–46.

3. Hyman B. Kaitz, "Experience of the Past: The National Minimum," in U.S. Department of Labor, *Youth Unemployment and Minimum Wages* (Washington: Government Printing Office, 1970).

4. Hugh Folk, "The Problem of Youth Unemployment," in *The Transition from School to Work* (Princeton, N.J.: Princeton University Press, 1968), pp. 76–107.

5. Michael C. Lovell, "The Minimum Wage, Teenage Umemployment, and the Business Cycle," *Western Economic Journal,* December 1972, pp. 414–27.

6. Robert S. Goldfarb, "The Policy Content of Quantitative Minimum Wage Research," *Annual Proceedings of the Industrial Relations Research Association* (Madison, Wis.: Industrial Relations Research Association, 1974), pp. 264–65.

7. New York State Department of Labor, Division of Research and Statistics, *Economic Effects of Minimum Wages: The New York State Retail Trade Order of 1957–58,* (Albany, N.Y.: 1964), pp. 23, 80–83, 112–14.

8. N. Arnold Tolles, "American Minimum Wage Laws: Their Purposes and Results," *Annual Proceedings of the Industrial Relations Research Association* (Madison, Wis.: Industrial Relations Research Association, 1959), pp. 116–133.

9. Edward M. Gramlich, "Impact of Minimum Wages on Other Wages, Employment, and Family Incomes," *Brookings Papers on Economic Activity,* 2:1976, pp. 442–43.

10. John D. Owen, "Why Part-Time Workers Tend to be in Low-Wage Jobs," *Monthly Labor Review,* June 1978, pp. 11–13.

11. Marvin Kosters and Finis Welch, "The Effects of Minimum Wages on the Distribution of Changes in Aggregate Employment," *American Economic Review,* June 1972, pp. 323–32.

12. John W. Kendrick, *Understanding Productivity* (Baltimore: Johns Hopkins University Press, 1977), pp. 53–54.

13. Lester C. Thurow, *Youth Unemployment* (New York: Rockefeller Foundation, 1977), p. 18.

14. Finis Welch, "Minimum Wage Legislation in the United States," *Economic Inquiry,* September 1974, pp. 285–318; Frederic Siskind, "Minimum Wage Legislation in the United States, Comment," *Economic Inquiry,* January 1977; Finis Welch, "Minimum Wage Legislation in the United States, Reply," *Economic Inquiry,* January 1977; and Finis Welch, *Minimum Wages: Issues and Evidence* (Washington: American Enterprise Institute, 1978), pp. 28–32.

15. Jacob Mincer, "Unemployment Effects of Minimum Wages," *Journal of Political Economy,* August 1976, pp. S87–S104.

16. James F. Regan, Jr., "Minimum Wages and the Youth Labor Market," *Review of Economics and Statistics,* May 1977, pp. 129–36.

17. Martin Feldstein, "The Economics of the New Unemployment," *Public Interest,* Fall 1973, pp. 3–42.

18. J. Wilson Mixon, Jr., "The Minimum Wage and Voluntary Labor Mobility," *Industrial and Labor Relations Review,* October 1978, pp. 69–71.

19. Albert Zucker, "Minimum Wages and the Long Run Elasticity of Demand for Low-Wage Labor," *Quarterly Journal of Economics,* May 1973, pp. 267–77.

20. Terence F. Kelly, *Two Policy Questions Regarding the Minimum Wage* (Washington: Urban Institute, 1976), pp. 19–20.

21. Edward Gramlich, op. cit., pp. 409–451.

22. Ibid., p. 443.

Chapter 5

1. U.S. Congress, House Committee on Education and Labor, Subcommittee on Labor Standards, *Hearings on 1977 Amendments to the Fair Labor Standards Act* (Washington: Government Printing Office, 1977), p. 5.

2. Ibid., p. 475.

3. *Congressional Quarterly,* March 26, 1977, p. 424.

4. *Congressional Quarterly,* June 8, 1977, p. 508.

5. U.S. Congress, House Committee on Education and Labor, op. cit., pp. 346–49.

6. Philip E. Graves, Ronald J. Krumm, and George S. Tolley, "New Estimates of the Effect of Minimum Wages on the United States Economy Updating Measures of Sensitivity to Minimum Wage Increases" (Chicago: University of Chicago, 1977, processed), pp. 4–6.

7. U.S. Congress, Senate Committee on Human Resources, Subcommittee on Labor, *Hearings on the 1977 Amendments to the Fair Labor Standards Act* (Washington: Government Printing Office, 1977), pp. 12–13.

8. U.S. Congress, House Committee on Education and Labor, op. cit., p. 290.

9. *Congressional Quarterly,* June 8, 1977, p. 508.

10. U.S. Congress, House Committee on Education and Labor, *Report on the Fair Labor Standards Amendments of 1977* (Washington: Government Printing Office, 1977), pp. 9–10.

11. Ibid., pp. 14–15.

12. Ibid., pp. 16–17.

13. William G. Whittaker and Charles V. Ciccone, *The Fair Labor Standards Act Amendments in the Ninety-Fifth Congress* (Washington: Congressional Research Service, 1977), p. 21.

14. *Congressional Record* (daily edition), September 15, 1977, p. H-9433.

15. *Congressional Record* (daily edition), September 15, 1977, p. H-9437.

16. *Congressional Record* (daily edition), October 7, 1977, p. S-16670.

17. *Congressional Record* (daily edition), July 26, 1977, p. H-7812.

18. Walter E. Williams, *Youth and Minority Unemployment* (Washington: Joint Economic Committee, 95th Congress, first session), p.. 4; and U.S. Congressional Budget Office, *The Teenage Unemployment Problem: What Are the Options?* (Washington: Government Printing Office, 1976), pp. 69–70.

19. Arvil V. Adams and Garth L. Mangum, *The Lingering Crisis of Youth Unemployment* (Kalamazoo, Mich.: W. E. Upjohn Institute for Employment Research, 1978), pp. 102–3.

20. Cited in William G. Whittaker, *The Fair Labor Standards Act of 1977: Floor Action in the House of Representatives* (Washington: Congressional Research Service, 1977), p. 12.

21. U.S. Congress, House Committee on Education and Labor, Subcommittee on Labor Standards, *Hearings on 1971 Amendments to the Fair Labor Standards Act* (Washington: Government Printing Office, 1971), pp. 123–25.

22. U.S. Congress, Senate Committee on Human Resources, op. cit., p. 95.

23. Letter from Secretary of Labor F. Ray Marshall to Senator Jacob K. Javits, August 16, 1977, p. 51.

24. *Congressional Record* (daily edition), October 7, 1977, p. S-16665.

25. U.S. Congress, Senate Committee on Human Resources, *Report on the 1977 Amendments to the Fair Labor Standards Act* (Washington: Government Printing Office, 1977), p. 26.

26. *The Employment and Training Report of the President, 1977* (Washington: Government Printing Office, 1977), p. 252.

27. William G. Whittaker, *The Fair Labor Standards Act Amendments of 1977: Analysis of Proposed Floor Amendments to H.R. 3744 to Provide For a Subminimum Wage for Certain Classes of Workers—Bill Analysis and Pro-Con Discussion* (Washington: Congressional Research Service, 1977), p. 16.

28. *Daily Labor Report*, March 16, 1977, p. E-1.

29. Lane Kirkland, "Minimum Wage Boost a Matter of Justice," *AFL-CIO News*, September 3, 1977, pp. 1–3.

30. *Congressional Record* (daily edition), September 15, 1977, p. H-9457.

31. *Wall Street Journal*, September 16, 1977, p. 2.

32. *Congressional Record* (daily edition), October 7, 1977, pp. S-16648–49.

33. *Congressional Record* (daily edition), September 15, 1977, p. H-9439.

34. The eight members of the commission are Gerald M. Feder, an attorney, chairman; William D. Byrum, executive vice president of the Michigan Cattlemen's Association; James O'Hara, a former congressman from Michigan; S. Warner Robinson, chairman of the board and chief executive officer of G.C.

Murphy Company; Clara F. Schloss, consultant on minimum wages to the AFL-CIO; Michael L. Wachter, University of Pennsylvania; Phyllis Ann Wallace, Massachusetts Institute of Technology; and Sandra L. Willett, executive vice president of the National Consumers League.

Chapter 6

1. Voltaire, *Candide* (New York: Random House, 1948), pp. 147–48.

2. Lester Thurow, *Youth Unemployment* (New York: Rockefeller Foundation, 1977), pp. 21–22.

3. John Bishop, *The Administration of a Wage Rate Subsidy* (Madison, Wis.: Institute for Research on Poverty, 1977), pp. 2–5.

4. John Bishop and Robert Lerman, "Wage Rate Subsidies for Income Maintenance and Job Creation," in Robert Taggart. ed. *Job Creation: What Works?* (Salt Lake City, Utah: Olympus Publishing Company, 1977), pp. 64–65.

5. Minimum Wage Study Commission, "Transcript of the Public Meeting Held in Washington, D.C.," August 22, 1978, (processed), p. 91.

172

List of Figures

174

Index

175

Library of Congress Cataloging in Publication Data

Levitan, Sar A.
  More than subsistence.

  (Policy studies in employment and welfare;
no. 34)
  Includes bibliographical references and index.
  1. Wages—Minimum wage—United States.
2. Poor—Employment—United States. I. Belous,
Richard S., joint author. II. Title.
HD4918.L45   331.2'1   79-11688
ISBN 0-8018-2251-3
ISBN 0-8018-2274-2 (pbk.)